KINGDOM LEADERSHIP

Developing Effective Leaders
for the Kingdom of Heaven

NATHAN PORTER

Ark House Press
arkhousepress.com

Copyright Act 1968 (Cth), © 2024 by Nathan Porter, Adelaide, Australia
All Rights Reserved

All rights reserved. Apart from any fair dealing for the purpose of study, research, criticism, or review, as permitted under the Copyright Act, no part may be reproduced by any process without written permission.

Unless otherwise indicated, all Scripture quotations are from The ESV® Bible (The Holy Bible, English Standard Version®), copyright © 2001 by Crossway, a publishing ministry of Good News Publishers. Used by permission. All rights reserved.

Cataloguing in Publication Data:
Title: Kingdom Leadership: Developing Effective Leaders for the Kingdom of Heaven
ISBN: 978-1-7637720-8-3 (pbk)
Subjects: REL108030   RELIGION / Christian Living / Leadership & Mentoring; REL012090   RELIGION / Christian Living / Professional Growth; REL074000 RELIGION / Christian Ministry / Pastoral Resources;

Design by initiateagency.com

DEDICATION

To my wife, whose strength, support, and encouragement during our shared trials and difficulties are blessings beyond measure. Without this support, I would not have been able to complete this book and bring it to life.

To my daughter and son, whose presence brings joy and light to every morning, and whose blessings have enriched my life and that of their mother beyond our wildest dreams.

Finally, to God: In every moment of my uncertainty, fatigue, weakness, or doubt, I thank You for Your encouraging words.

"…fear not, for I am with you; be not dismayed, for I am your God; I will strengthen you, I will help you, I will uphold you with my righteous right hand." Isaiah 41:10

CONTENTS

Preface vii
Introduction xi
Chapter One: Basis for Purposeful Kingdom Leadership 1
Chapter Two: Applying Kingdom Leadership 25
Chapter Three: Restructuring your Kingdom Leadership 49
Chapter Four: Your Seed and Passion 70
Chapter Five: World Concepts of Leadership 80
Chapter Six: Fruits of Kingdom Leadership 100
Chapter Seven: Kingdom Leadership Summary 137
Acknowledgements 143
Endnotes 145

PREFACE

In this book, my objective is to explore a range of leadership concepts that have profoundly shaped my understanding. Drawing from personal experiences, rigorous studies, and thoughtful reflections, I aim to provide a comprehensive look at leadership principles. The force behind my original exploration of leadership stems from a deep-seated desire to comprehend its significance and influence in shaping individuals and societies.

My intent is to illustrate both the theoretical foundations and practical applications of Kingdom Leadership and offer valuable guidance for aspiring leaders and those interested in the dynamics of leading others. My many years of exploring this topic have cultivated a deep understanding of what my purpose as a leader within the Kingdom of Heaven is. I hope for you to attain the same understanding of your purpose as a leader in the Kingdom of Heaven.

Throughout history, humanity has sought leaders to guide and direct them, to find ways to improve their lives. As I searched for understanding, I could not help but feel that the world's way of leadership was lacking. The prevailing concepts seemed more focused on control rather than the development or betterment of others. This led me to seek understanding and explore, more deeply, the biblical concepts of leadership and how they differ from what we have become accustomed to.

In seeking to better understand God's original intent, it became clear that His desire for our leadership was to operate within His Kingdom. Through Kingdom Leadership, I came to an understanding of how God desires for society to be transformed and impacted for His glory and the expansion of His Kingdom. When we turn our focus toward Him and seek His Kingdom first, our leadership adopts a perspective that is markedly different from that of the world.

I am compelled to share what I have learned, to impart knowledge and to inspire others to recognize their own leadership potential, regardless of background, age, or perceived limitations. My main goal is to demonstrate how our individual leadership, perfectly placed and designed by God, enables us to successfully strive in unison in expanding the Kingdom of Heaven.

One aspect is to define leadership within the framework of its original intent as I perceive it through the lens of God's perspective. I studied what the Bible had to say in addition to reading various books by Christian authors. Through this process, I began to piece together the concept of Kingdom Leadership. While many authors offered amazing insights around biblical leadership styles, I could not find a book that compared their Christian leadership concepts with those taught by the world.

I delved further, making comparing worldly leadership concepts with biblical teachings to truly grasp their differences. I researched deeper into biblical principles and scripture and saw a clear comparative framework emerge. Through this process, I received a revelation from God, realizing that He has already instilled leadership within me, and His desire is for me to develop it according to His purpose for my life. While some of these concepts may resonate with your existing understanding of leadership, others may challenge your mindset, offering new insights and perspectives.

PREFACE

Before going into the exploration of Kingdom Leadership, allow me to share a bit about my background. I hail from the outer suburbs of Melbourne, Australia, where I spent my formative years before embarking on a journey that would lead me to living and working overseas. My experiences range from working in construction to holding management roles in international developments in Myanmar, where I engaged with leaders from diverse backgrounds and cultures, at the pinnacle of business. These roles opened doors for me to sit with world banks, global conglomerates, and various other international companies, as well as small business owners and contractors.

During my time in Myanmar, I served as a director, then Chairperson, of an international non-governmental organization (INGO) focused on peacebuilding in conflict-affected areas. This experience significantly enriched my understanding of leadership in the realms of social impact and humanitarian work. Alongside my wife, I had the opportunity through this organization to encourage children who had been rescued from slavery, sex trafficking, or abandonment. We also supported the implementation of WASH (Water, Sanitation, and Hygiene) programs in communities to promote health and sanitation, and distributed food to marginalized regions.

Upon returning to Australia, and settling in Adelaide, I transitioned into Human Resources, where I have been able to further explore and develop my leadership skills in new and dynamic ways. This role has allowed me to put into practice the leadership concepts I have cultivated, successfully supporting my employer and colleagues. My promotions serve as a clear indicator of my success in implementing these leadership principles.

These diverse experiences in international property development, coupled with my humanitarian work, have given me a comprehensive understanding of the impact of leadership across different facets of society. From the upper echelons of international business to the lives of those forgotten and marginalized, I have gained profound insights into how leadership can affect various aspects of life.

My academic journey has been equally diverse, spanning seven years of formal study across Australian universities, culminating in a Bachelor of Business with a Finance Major, and a Master of Business Administration (MBA) with a specialization in leadership. These studies, along with my real-world experiences and my quest to understand the essence of various leadership structures, have shaped my perspective. From this learning experience, I have a strong passion for sharing my knowledge to inspire others to recognize their own Kingdom Leadership.

As you delve into each chapter, I will invite you to take moments for reflection, allowing the ideas presented to resonate and interact with your own perceptions of leadership. I encourage you to engage in this process with an open mind, welcoming the opportunity for growth and transformation.

Moreover, I urge you to test these concepts against the timeless wisdom found in the word of God. As you explore these pages, consider how each idea aligns with God's intentions and principles. Let the Holy Spirit lead you through God's Word and uncover its significance for you. Ultimately, it is my hope that this book serves as a catalyst for deeper exploration and understanding of Kingdom Leadership in light of God's truth.

As you embark on this journey, I invite you to open your heart and mind to the Kingdom Leadership structure guided by the Father's principles within the Bible. May this exploration enrich your understanding and empower you to embrace your role as a leader in God's Kingdom.

INTRODUCTION

Welcome to "Kingdom Leadership: Developing Effective Leaders for the Kingdom of Heaven." In the vast landscape of leadership literature, countless theories, models, and methodologies abound, each one offering their own perspective on what it means to lead effectively. However, amidst the plethora of leadership paradigms, one often overlooked, yet profoundly impactful lens through which to view leadership, is the Kingdom of Heaven.

In this book, we embark on a journey to explore the origins and essence of leadership from a biblical standpoint, delving into timeless principles that transcend cultural and temporal boundaries. As we navigate through the chapters, we will uncover the rich tapestry of leadership, weaved through scripture from Genesis to the New Testament, pertaining to the Kingdom of Heaven on earth, exploring concepts such as "Basileia" (kingdom and dominion), leadership through purpose, and the transformative power of Jesus' leadership example.

The Kingdom of Heaven represents the sovereign structure of authority established by God, reigning over all creation from His heavenly realm. This divine order finds its earthly manifestation within every believer through their relationship with Jesus Christ. This is evident from the Gospel of Luke when Jesus is talking of the Kingdom of Heaven.

"the Kingdom of God is in the midst of you." Luke 17:21

Jesus teaches that the Kingdom of Heaven is not only a future promise but a present reality that dwells within every believer who has accepted Him as their Lord. This intimate presence of the Kingdom is a result of Jesus reigning as King in the hearts and lives of His followers. Wherever Jesus goes, His Kingdom accompanies Him, influencing and transforming individuals and communities through His divine presence and authority. This truth emphasizes the personal and pervasive nature of the Kingdom of Heaven, shaping the beliefs, values, and actions of those who walk in fellowship with Christ. Therefore, wherever Christians go, they carry the Kingdom of Heaven with them.

As a community of believers, the Church embodies the presence of the Kingdom of Heaven. When united as the Body of Christ, the Church has the power to effect societal change. As Christians, we operate within the Kingdom of Heaven wherever we are—whether in the Church, our communities, or our families. Living out this reality means living a life aligned with the principles and values of the Kingdom of Heaven.

> *"For the Kingdom of God is not a matter of eating and drinking but of righteousness and peace and joy in the Holy Spirit." Romans 14:17*

This journey is not merely about acquiring knowledge or mastering skills; it is about undergoing a profound transformation—a shift in thinking, beliefs, convictions, attitudes, perceptions, and behavior. By embracing the biblical Kingdom Leadership principles and structure presented in this book, and allowing yourself to be transformed, you will embark on a journey of self-discovery and personal growth, unlocking your full potential as a leader.

Our exploration includes an examination of concepts such as self-worth, self-esteem, and self-concept, recognizing the intrinsic value and potential within everyone as a Kingdom Leader. From there, we delve into the seeds of leadership planted within us, igniting a passion to succeed and make a difference in the world. Reflecting on and understanding these concepts will empower you with a strong self-belief in your purpose as a leader within the Kingdom of Heaven.

To understand the evolution of worldly concepts of leadership throughout history, we will journey through the corridors of time, exploring the insights of influential thinkers such as Plato, Machiavelli, and Carlyle, and contemporary scholars like Burns, Weber, and Hershey-Blanchard. Through this historical lens, we gain a deeper appreciation for the complexities and nuances of leadership dynamics. A comparison of these worldly leadership concepts with the Kingdom Leadership structure is shared, to provide clarity on the distinct differences between the world's concept of leadership and the biblical Kingdom Leadership concept.

As we progress, we will uncover fruits of effective Kingdom Leadership, from creativity and time management to teamwork, patience, accountability, integrity, self-development, and discipline. Each section offers practical insights and strategies to cultivate these essential qualities, empowering you to lead with purpose and authenticity.

I am deeply passionate about learning about the Kingdom of Heaven and its profound significance for God and the world. This passion has driven me to dedicate many years to studying leadership, drawing insights from the Bible, numerous esteemed authors, and various scholarly articles. Through this extensive exploration, I have developed a robust understanding of the critical role leadership plays in His Church.

My journey has been enriched by delving into the teachings of the Bible and discovering timeless principles of Kingdom Leadership. I have gained valuable perspectives from contemporary Christian authors who have written extensively on leadership within a spiritual context. Articles and theological discussions have further enhanced my comprehension, providing a well-rounded view of what it means to lead in alignment with God's will in His Kingdom.

A pivotal moment in my journey was receiving the revelation from God that illuminated His divine intent for us as Kingdom Leaders. This revelation provided clarity and purpose, enabling me to understand the unique call and responsibility bestowed upon us. It underscored the importance of leading with integrity, compassion, and a steadfast commitment to advancing His Kingdom on earth.

Through this divine insight, I have come to realize that Kingdom Leadership is not merely about holding positions of authority but about serving others, guiding them with wisdom, and embodying the values of the Kingdom of Heaven in every aspect of our lives. This understanding fuels my passion and commitment to sharing this knowledge with others, inspiring them to embrace their own roles as Kingdom Leaders and to fulfill God's vision for His Church and the world.

So, are you ready to embark on this transformative journey? Are you ready to shift your perspective, elevate your leadership, and make a lasting impact in your sphere of influence? If so, let us journey together into the heart of Kingdom Leadership, guided by the timeless wisdom of the Kingdom of Heaven perspective.

CHAPTER ONE

BASIS FOR PURPOSEFUL KINGDOM LEADERSHIP

ORIGIN OF LEADERSHIP

Understanding the principles of the Kingdom of Heaven and how a kingdom operates is essential to our journey to becoming Kingdom Leaders. Every individual has the potential to influence and guide others from a posture of leadership, regardless of their formal title or position.

Kingdom principles equip us to effectively extend our influence on earth for the higher purpose of expanding God's Kingdom. Jesus was the perfect example of a pragmatic and compassionate leader. He had many teachings, proclamations, and declarations of power and authority, which He imparted throughout His earthly ministry, focusing heavily on the Kingdom of Heaven.

As His leadership style is one that, as followers of Christ, we should wish to emulate, it is important to develop our leadership abilities in our daily life to ensure we understand our crucial function as a part of the Church, as Kingdom Leaders.

Why do we need to extend the Kingdom of Heaven on earth?

> *"And Jesus came and said to them, 'All authority in heaven and on earth has been given to me. Go therefore and make disciples of all nations, baptizing them in the name of the Father and of the Son and of the Holy Spirit, teaching them to observe all that I have commanded you. And behold, I am with you always, to the end of the age.'" Matthew 28:18-20*

When Jesus went to heaven, his last command marked His commission to go forth and advance the Kingdom of Heaven, the Kingdom of God, here on earth. It reflected the impartation of His ministry into His people, His Church, to go and teach people of all nations what He has commanded to observe.

Jesus called His followers to actively participate in expanding the Kingdom of Heaven, and not passively wait for others to advance it. Engaging with the expansion of the Kingdom of Heaven is a responsibility that each Kingdom Leader must embrace, regardless of circumstances or locations. To effectively fulfill Jesus' calling, it is essential to understand the Kingdom Leadership He has cultivated and endowed in everyone.

Whether it is leading a team, inspiring followers, or setting an example for others, every person can make a positive impact and contribute to the collective progress of the Kingdom of God. Collective progress refers to the advancement and improvement of a group, community, or society, rather than focusing on individual success. It highlights the importance of working together and supporting one another to achieve common goals and shared benefits. In this instance, it is working to the collective progress of advancing the Kingdom of God.

For Kingdom Leaders to actively engage in shaping the world around them and fostering positive change, they must recognize and embrace the inherent leadership potential that God has placed within each of them. Leadership is not solely defined by holding a specific role in society or church culture but rather by the actions, attitudes, and values exhibited in our everyday interactions.

To better understand Kingdom Leadership and its distinct differences from worldly concepts of leadership, we need to first have a basic understanding of the worldly concepts. Across cultures and throughout history, leadership has been a cornerstone of human society, emerging from the need for organization, direction, and guidance within groups and communities. The world's view of leadership as a mechanism of control over society differs significantly from Kingdom Leadership, where it is about leading within the talents, gifts, or abilities God has placed in us to serve His Kingdom.

One can trace the roots of leadership to early human societies, where individuals with certain qualities, such as strength, wisdom, or charisma, naturally emerged as leaders due to their ability to inspire and influence others. These ideas about what constitutes a leader have unintentionally permeated into the Church, often leading to a departure from God's original intent.

Recognizing the distinction between Kingdom Leadership and the world's definition of leadership is crucial for realigning with God's intent. Throughout history, from the era of the Ancient Greeks to the present day, several common beliefs about leadership have persisted:

1. Leadership is an innate trait, possessed only by those born with certain skills; it is not something that can be developed or acquired by most individuals.

2. True leaders are not created through training or education; rather, they inherently possess the right combination of traits or attributes that predispose them to leadership roles.
3. Leadership is often perceived as a birthright, reserved for individuals born into powerful or influential families who inherit their leadership positions.
4. Charisma is considered essential for effective leadership, as leaders must possess the ability to captivate and engage others through their magnetic personality and charm.
5. In some contexts, leadership is associated with the use of force or coercion to assert dominance and control over others.
6. Leadership is believed to be attainable only through specialized training or education, and individuals without formal instruction in leadership principles are not considered capable of assuming leadership roles.

These beliefs reflect various cultural norms, historical contexts, and societal expectations surrounding leadership, shaping the way leadership is perceived and practiced in different communities and organizations.

Leadership is indeed a complex and intangible concept that poses challenges for society to define. Unlike tangible assets, it encompasses a blend of qualities and behaviors that can vary greatly depending on context and perspective. This diversity within leadership across society makes it difficult to construct a singular definition of leadership that fully captures its essence.

The abundance of diverse concepts and theories about leadership worldwide reflects its complexity. While society has tried to define leadership and how it can be obtained, individuals fail to recognize leadership as a crucial framework to operate from even when it is beneficial to embody leadership as a lifestyle that benefits the Kingdom of God.

Many of the world's concepts of leadership focus on exerting control, directing, influencing, manipulating, dictating, and even subverting humanity. Some concepts of leadership revolve around imposing one's will and desires on others, dictating how others should live for the sole purpose of elevating the leader's own status and agenda. Consequently, corruption and manipulation can readily infiltrate a leader's behavior, whether in governments, corporations, or within the Church.

While through the study and contemplation of scripture one can discover and recognize leadership as a crucial framework to operate from, in an alignment with their divine calling or purpose bestowed by God, many individuals fail to reach this understanding. As a result, many Christians lack a clearly defined framework for Kingdom Leadership, which is why sharing this knowledge as a tool to enable and empower Christians is essential.

Genesis serves as a starting point to explore the biblical concept of leadership, illustrating foundational structures and principles.

> *"Then God said, 'Let us make man in our image, after our likeness.* **And let them have dominion** *over the fish of the sea and over the birds of the heavens and over the livestock and over all the earth and over every creeping thing that creeps on the earth.' So, God created man in his own image, in the image of God he created him; male and female he created them." Genesis 1:26-27 (bold added)*

In the passage above, scripture makes it clear that humans have dominion and leadership over all other creations on earth. There is no indication that humans are granted dominion or leadership over each other; rather, the focus is on dominion over all other earthly creations.

God's intention is not for humans to exercise control over each other, but rather to guide, encourage, support, and uplift one another. While God desires us to lead and make a positive impact for His Kingdom, societal concepts of leadership can infiltrate our thinking, leading leaders to impose controls or dominance over others' lives.

Genesis 1 offers insight into God's wisdom and intentional establishment of the natural and spiritual order of the universe. God begins by separating light from darkness, followed by the separation of the waters to establish the Heavens and the Earth. After separating the waters, God creates the dry land, forming earth amidst the waters.

Following the creation of earth, God populates it with plants, fruits, and seeds, ensuring the continuity of vegetation life. He then establishes the sun, moon, and stars to govern time and provide light for the earth. God then creates animals, including birds in the air and fish in the sea. Only after creating all of this, God proceeds to create humanity.

Why create all these things first and then create humanity? If God created humanity first prior to creating the birds, animals, and sea creatures and all the wonderous plants, there would have been no purpose for humanity on earth.

From scripture, we learn that God knows everything from beginning to end. Within His infinite knowledge, He knew what humanity would require even before He created Adam and placed him on earth. God is intentional in all He does; He created the world through His spoken word, establishing purpose first. We see this intentionality in the order of creation over the first five and a half days, where everything was meticulously designed before humanity was introduced later on the sixth day. With this purpose in place, He then created humanity to fulfill it.

Humanity was created by God to exercise dominion over the earth, to care for it, guide it, and provide leadership to it according to God's plan. God created humanity to assume a leadership role over all His creations, nurturing, developing, and promoting His divine handiwork.

In Genesis 2:5-7, we read:

> *"When no bush of the field was yet in the land and no small plant of the field had yet sprung up – for the Lord God had not caused it to rain on the land, and* ***there was no man to work the ground****, and a mist was going up from the land and was watering the whole face of the ground – then the Lord God formed the man of dust from the ground and breathed into his nostrils the breath of life, and the man became a living creature."* (Bold added)

The work that God intends for humanity is not merely the daily job we engage in, but rather a broader responsibility of leadership, stewardship and care for His creation. It is the work that God ordained for us from the very beginning, as described in Genesis 1.

God ordained humanity to provide leadership and stewardship over the earth, so He waited until He created man and breathed life into his body before allowing the earth to fully flourish according to His divine plan.

Indeed, leadership was a part of God's intended design for humanity, as evidenced by the creation narrative in Genesis. However, this leadership was not intended for the control of each other but rather for humans to exercise Kingdom Leadership and influence over earth for God's glory. Living a life of Kingdom Leadership for God's glory means setting aside personal wants and desires for personal glory, to focus on unveiling God's splendor, majesty, and greatness for the world to see and know. God entrusted humanity with the responsibility to care for and preserve His creation, desiring that we could enjoy the earth in the manner He intended.

The deviation from the intended access to Kingdom Leadership occurred with the fall of humanity. When the forbidden fruit was consumed, which is when Adam and Eve consumed something they desired that was not permissible to indulge in, sin entered the world and God's plan and a purpose for both the world and humanity changed. With the entrance of sin into the world, there was a shift in how God would fulfill His plan and purpose, and enable people to operate as Kingdom Leaders, ultimately leading to Jesus coming to earth.

Because God is omniscient, He knew that sin would enter the world. Before sin entered, God had a direct connection with humanity, as seen in Scripture when He walked in the garden with Adam and Eve. Through this intimate connection, God imparted the understanding of Kingdom Leadership that we needed to fulfill His plan and purpose directly.

When sin entered the world, God could no longer reside around the presence of this unforgiven sin, as He cannot coexist with it. This is affirmed by scriptures in Psalms and Habakkuk.

> *"For you are not a God who delights in wickedness; evil may not dwell with you."* Psalm 5:4

> *"You who are of purer eyes than to see evil and cannot look at wrong..."* Habakkuk 1:13

To bridge this separation between Himself and humanity caused by sin, the Ark of the Covenant was created to allow His presence on earth. Subsequently, detailed instructions were given for the construction of the first temple, designed to provide a place for God's presence on earth while maintaining separation from the sin that permeates the world.

To reestablish a connection with all humanity and transcend the limitations of the temple, enabling His overarching plan to succeed, God sent Jesus to make the ultimate sacrifice. Through Christ's death as the perfect sacrifice, the power of sin was broken, granting people forgiveness through Him, and God's presence could be released from the temple to all people when the curtain tore.

This reflects the intention from God to ensure that His original plan and structure regarding His relationship with us, aimed at providing Kingdom Leadership over the earth, was still accessible as desired.

Despite the change brought about by sin, God's overarching purpose for humanity remains unchanged. However, there is a difference now in how humans can access, obtain, and exercise leadership in the way God intended, allowing them to ultimately influence their surroundings for God's purpose. In the Garden of Eden, God walked personally with Adam and Eve and there was direct access to Him. Now, God walks with those who recognize Jesus Christ as their Lord and Savior, enabling them to access, obtain, and exercise Kingdom Leadership as He intended.

KINGDOM OF HEAVEN ON EARTH

Following the Fall of Man, the bond between Heaven and Earth was severed, and we ceased to walk in harmonious unity with the Father. God's desire for us to collaborate with Him in influencing the earth remained unchanged, yet He knew the need for a different approach. Jesus was sent to earth to facilitate, through His sacrifice, a direct pathway back to the Father. By believing in Christ Jesus, we can attain forgiveness and reestablish our connection to the Father, thereby realigning with His intended purpose for us on earth.

Initially, the earth mirrored the thoughts of God, and Heaven and Earth functioned in perfect harmony. Prior to pronouncing the words that brought life into existence, God had already envisioned in His mind the form it would take. In Genesis 1:26-27, we learn that God reflected on creating humanity. He envisioned the form humanity would take and the dominion we would have. He then fashioned us with His hands, as described in Isaiah 64:8, like a potter taking clay and molding it with their hands.

Unlike the rest of creation, where God spoke it into existence, He personally shaped humanity according to His design and intent, forming us with His hands. To further grasp the concept that God had us in mind and thought about us before creating the world, we can find joy in Ephesians 1:4, where it states:

> *"even as he chose us in him before the foundation of the world, that we should be holy and blameless before him."*

From this we can be encouraged that God saw us, that He thought on us, before He started laying the foundations of the world and speaking it into creation. God desired a direct connection to humanity, and with this, a connection between Heaven and Earth.

With sin disrupting this connection, Heaven and Earth ceased to operate in seamless harmony, leading to humanity's gradual estrangement from God across generations. This shift away from God is evident early in Genesis, as Cain and his descendants turn from Him. Throughout the Old Testament, the Israelites also fluctuate in their position and relationship with God. This trend continues today within Christianity, as nations founded on Christian principles are increasingly moving away from God as a foundational element.

In the present era, we find ourselves amidst a profound loss of identity and a breakdown in the very structure of life that God originally breathed into creation. We are witnessing the promotion of behaviors and concepts that God has deemed sinful as virtuous, while that which God considers good is now often regarded as shameful. Despite this, God has not forsaken His purpose for humanity on earth; He still desires for us to mirror His image here on earth.

To fulfill His purpose on earth, God sent Jesus to restore the severed connection. There is significant emphasis and teaching on what Jesus has accomplished for us through His birth, death, and resurrection. We are well acquainted with the stories of the individuals He healed from diseases, those He liberated from demonic possession, and the parables He shared.

We must delve deeper into the significance of the "Kingdom of Heaven on Earth" and grasp why it held such paramount importance to Jesus for Him to have spent so much time preaching about it wherever he went. However, we often overlook this central message that Jesus, as well as John the Baptist, fervently preached wherever they went. We must comprehend how this concept of the Kingdom of Heaven on earth aligns with God's original intent for humanity and the type of leadership He envisioned for us.

In the four Gospels, we encounter numerous instances of Jesus and John the Baptist teaching about the Kingdom of Heaven. Early in the book of Matthew, it refers to John the Baptist preaching in the wilderness of Judea about the Kingdom of Heaven.

> "In those days John the Baptist came preaching in the wilderness of Judea, 'repent, for the kingdom of heaven is at hand'." Matthew 3:1-2

John is recognized as the voice mentioned in the prophecy of Isaiah 40:3-4, which speaks of a voice in the wilderness preparing the way for the

Lord. This scripture is significant as it marks the beginning of the transformative shift God desires to reestablish the connection between Heaven and Earth.

In the Garden of Eden, God walked in harmony with humanity. After humanity fell, they began to create their own forms of governance to rule the earth. These governments shifted focus from God to humanity as the central figure. With John's preaching in the wilderness and his emphasis on the Kingdom of Heaven, we witness God's movement to establish His Kingdom on earth.

Following on from John, Jesus consistently preached about the arrival of the Kingdom of Heaven wherever He went. This concept was foundational to Jesus, as He desired for many people to understand that they would have access to something profoundly powerful.

> *"And Jesus went throughout all the cities and villages, teaching in their synagogues and proclaiming the gospel of the kingdom and healing every disease and every affliction." Matthew 9:35*

From this scripture, it is evident that Jesus embarked on extensive journeys to engage with people in various cities and villages. He actively participated in their communities, frequenting their synagogues where He passionately taught and proclaimed the Kingdom of Heaven. Beyond teaching, Jesus demonstrated the compassionate nature of His ministry by healing those afflicted with diseases and various forms of suffering.

The miracles of healing that Jesus performed were not only demonstrations of His compassion and power but also strategic acts to emphasize the imminent arrival of the Kingdom of Heaven. By healing the sick, restoring sight to the blind, and freeing people from afflictions, Jesus sought to capture the attention and hearts of those witnessing these miracles.

These miraculous signs were intended to create a fertile ground for His teachings about the Kingdom, prompting people to listen attentively and receive His message with openness and faith. Jesus used these acts of healing not only to alleviate suffering but also to invite people into a deeper understanding and anticipation of God's reign and sovereignty that was unfolding among them.

Emphasizing the significance of the Kingdom of Heaven, Jesus desired for others to share the news about it. His initial instructions for going out and preaching about the Kingdom were directed to His disciples.

> *"And He called the twelve together and gave them power and authority over all demons and to cure diseases, and He sent them out to proclaim the kingdom of God and to heal."*
> Luke 9:1-2

From this scripture, we see that Jesus first bestowed upon them the power and authority over all demons and the ability to cure diseases. This is crucial because without His power and authority, our efforts would be futile. After granting them this power and authority, Jesus sent the disciples out with two primary missions: to proclaim the Kingdom of God and to heal. This scripture also highlights the first time Jesus equips humanity to become Kingdom Leaders.

There is often a tendency to emphasize the healing aspect of this scripture while overlooking the proclamation of the Kingdom. The physical restoration of a person's body is tangible and visible, sparking excitement. In contrast, the Kingdom of Heaven is sometimes viewed as an abstract concept that can be challenging to grasp.

In this scripture, Jesus emphasizes the order of priorities: to proclaim the Kingdom of God as the primary message and healing as a subsequent action. This underscores His desire for people to grasp the profound truth and eternal impact of the Kingdom before experiencing physical healing. By prioritizing the proclamation of the Kingdom, Jesus directs attention to the transformative power and authority inherent in His message. The healing miracles that follow serve as tangible demonstrations of God's Kingdom breaking into the present reality, affirming His sovereignty and compassion. Thus, Jesus' instructions highlight the Kingdom's central role in His ministry, and to equip us as Kingdom Leaders.

Throughout His ministry, Jesus consistently taught to all who would listen, about the imminent arrival of the Kingdom of Heaven, as evident in these scriptures and many others found throughout the Gospels. How was the Kingdom of Heaven going to arrive, and how would heaven connect to earth to achieve this?

Jesus sacrificially laid down His life as the perfect offering, enabling humanity to reclaim our direct connection to the Father. Before Jesus' sacrifice, the only means of obtaining forgiveness from God and establishing a connection with Him was through the mediation of priests and the offering of animal sacrifices. During this period of human history, God's presence was confined within the temple, and people were unable to directly access Him.

Jesus revolutionized this concept, restoring humanity to a harmonious relationship with the Father, contingent upon our willingness to accept Christ as our Lord and Savior. Through Jesus' sacrificial offering for all humankind, there ceased to be a necessity for God to be confined to the temple, nor for people to seek Him solely within its confines.

All individuals gained direct access to Him, thereby enabling God, through Jesus, to reestablish the connection between Heaven and Earth. This newfound direct access facilitates the movement of the Kingdom of Heaven across the earth, fulfilling Jesus' teachings of its imminent arrival, realized through His death and resurrection. Jesus' death initiated the church on earth, establishing it as the primary gathering of His people within the Kingdom of Heaven on earth. To be effective in this, it is important to understand what a kingdom is.

A kingdom is a form of government. The Merriam-Webster dictionary online defines kingdom as, but not limited to:

1. a politically organized community or major territorial unit having a monarchical form of government headed by a king or queen
2. often capitalized
    a. the eternal kingship of God
    b. the realm in which God's will is fulfilled
3. a. a realm or region in which something is dominant
    b. an area or sphere in which one holds a preeminent position

As defined, a kingdom entails having dominion over the territory it encompasses. At its helm is a king or queen. A kingdom is characterized by a domain where a particular entity or ideology holds sway, and where an individual occupies a position of considerable significance or authority. God established the foundation of His Kingdom in the Garden of Eden by giving humanity dominion over the earth. In Jesus' parable in Matthew 25:31-46, discussing the final judgment, Jesus affirms the timing of the establishment of His Kingdom, as He invites those who will now share in it.

> *"Come, you who are blessed by my Father, inherit the kingdom prepared for you from the foundation of the world." Matthew 25:34*

Most intriguingly, the dictionary also defines a kingdom as the eternal kingship of God, where the fulfillment of God's will take precedence. Unlike other forms of government that may distribute power among various branches or officials, a kingdom is characterized by a singular individual who holds ultimate authority over all aspects of governance. This central figure possesses the highest level of power and control, ensuring that their will is enacted throughout the realm.

In the context of the Kingdom of Heaven, this supreme authority is God Himself. He reigns as the sovereign ruler, overseeing and directing every facet of the Kingdom. His will is paramount, guiding the principles, laws, and operations within this divine domain. The Kingdom of Heaven, therefore, is not merely a territory or realm; it is a manifestation of God's perfect and eternal rule, where His purposes and plans are fully realized. This divine governance reflects God's omnipotence, wisdom, and love, setting it apart from any earthly system of rule.

Jesus consistently taught about the imminent arrival and establishment of the Kingdom of Heaven throughout His ministry. His teachings emphasized that this Kingdom was not merely a future event but a present reality breaking into the world. Before His departure, Jesus entrusted His disciples with a crucial mission: to spread the Kingdom throughout the entire earth. This commission was more than a call to preach; it was a charge to actively participate in the unfolding of God's reign on earth.

The essence of this mission was to establish dominion over the earth, not in the sense of domination or control, but in the fulfillment of God's original plan for His Kingdom on earth.

BASILEIA - KINGDOM AND DOMINION

In delving into the nuances of the Greek language, particularly the term "Basileia," we uncover profound insights into the divine mandate entrusted to humanity from the very inception of creation. In its essence, "Basileia" encapsulates not only the concept of Kingdom but also dominion—a dual significance that reverberates throughout the biblical narrative.

Turning our gaze back to the genesis of human existence, we are reminded of the sacred charge bestowed upon humanity by the Creator Himself. In the pristine Garden of Eden, God granted Adam and Eve Basileia (dominion) over the earth, entrusting them with the stewardship and care of His creation. This Basileia was a manifestation of God's grace and favor, empowering humanity to exercise authority and influence over the natural world.

However, this divine mandate was marred by the tragic consequences of human disobedience. With the consumption of the forbidden fruit came the introduction of sin and its debilitating effects on the fabric of creation. Humanity's rebellion against God's sovereignty resulted in the forfeiture of their rightful dominion over the earth—a solemn reminder of the devastating consequences of disobedience and separation from the divine.

Yet, in the fullness of time, God, in His infinite mercy and grace, orchestrated a divine rescue mission to redeem and restore that which was lost. Through the life, death, and resurrection of Jesus Christ, humanity received the ultimate gift—the power and authority to reclaim their rightful Basileia over the earth and to establish the Kingdom of Heaven.

In the person of Jesus Christ, we behold the perfect embodiment of both Kingdom and Dominion. He not only proclaimed the arrival of the Kingdom of Heaven but also demonstrated its transformative power through His earthly ministry. His teachings, miracles, and acts of compassion ushered in a new era of divine rule—a reign characterized by justice, mercy, and redemption.

Through His sacrificial death on the cross, Jesus secured victory over sin and death, paving the way for the establishment of God's Kingdom here on earth. Through His resurrection and ascension, He conferred upon His followers the authority to continue His mission of reconciliation and restoration—a mission grounded in love, empowered by the Holy Spirit, and destined for the fulfillment of God's redemptive purposes.

As heirs of this divine inheritance, Christians are called to embrace their identity as ambassadors of the Kingdom of Heaven, entrusted with the sacred task of extending its borders and advancing its principles here on earth. With humility, courage, and unwavering faith, Christians join hands with the Savior in the ongoing work of building God's Kingdom—a Kingdom of love, peace, and righteousness that knows no end.

God's profound longing for the governance of the earth finds its ultimate expression in the concept of a Kingdom government—a divine order wherein He, as the sovereign King, reigns supreme, and wherein He graciously delegates authority to those who willingly acknowledge and submit to His lordship. This Kingdom government, rooted in God's absolute sovereignty and unwavering love, stands as the epitome of divine rule and divine justice.

Drawing parallels between the dynamics of earthly kingdoms and the expansion of the Kingdom of Heaven provides valuable insights into our role as leaders within God's divine order. Just as earthly kingdoms endeavor to extend their influence and dominion (Basileia) over foreign lands, so too are we called to propagate the Kingdom of Heaven to encompass "all the nations."

In ancient Greece, for instance, the city-states pioneered the development of an early form of democracy—a system of governance wherein power resided in the hands of the people, who collectively made decisions through participation in civic institutions and assemblies. This democratic experiment, though imperfect and limited in scope, laid the groundwork for the eventual evolution of democratic ideals and principles in later centuries.

Later, in the vast expanse of the Roman Empire, a different form of governance took root—the Republic. In this system, power was vested in elected officials and representative institutions, with a complex system of checks and balances designed to prevent the concentration of authority in the hands of any single individual or faction.

These two government structures were created by people to enable them to exert power and control over others. These individuals ruled with authority derived from their own strength, knowledge, or influence. Within these government structures, there was no allowance for any authority greater than themselves.

God did not intend for these governmental structures to govern His dominion; rather, He desired a Kingdom. In contrast to the governmental structures of ancient Greece or Rome, God desired individuals to function collectively rather than having the few rule over the many. He intended Himself to be the central focus within the Kingdom structure, not a few powerful individuals.

It is crucial to recognize that God transcends time, remaining constant and steadfast in His nature. When we note the consistent theme of "Basileia" in both Genesis, where it signifies the dominion granted to humanity at creation, and in the Gospels, where Jesus refers to the Kingdom of Heaven, we can discern God's enduring desire to be present with us on earth through His Kingdom.

Similar to any form of government, the Kingdom of Heaven necessitates leaders in various specialized fields to provide guidance and leadership on earth. Indeed, this is our purpose, and it is within this realm that each of us finds our leadership role.

The strategic approach employed by earthly kingdoms when establishing a presence in a foreign territory is, typically, to begin by founding a colony—a foothold from which their influence can gradually permeate the surrounding region. As the colony thrives and prospers in its initial city, its sphere of influence expands, reaching outwards to neighboring communities and cities. With each new outpost established, the kingdom's presence becomes more pronounced and its dominion more far-reaching.

This gradual process of expansion mirrors the organic growth and development of the Kingdom of Heaven on earth. As followers of Christ, we are entrusted with the task of spreading the Gospel message and advancing the principles of God's Kingdom to every corner of the globe. Just as a colony serves as a beacon of the kingdom's presence in a foreign land, so too are we called to be ambassadors of Christ, shining the light of His truth and love wherever we go.

Indeed, the Church stands as the colony of the Kingdom of Heaven on earth—a beacon of God's redemptive love and transformative power in a world marred by sin and brokenness. Unlike earthly kingdoms, whose expansion often relies on tactics of fear, division, and manipulation, the Kingdom of Heaven operates on principles of love, grace, and reconciliation.

Jesus Himself set the precedent for this distinct approach to Kingdom expansion through His teachings and example. He unequivocally emphasized the centrality of love in His ministry, declaring that love for one another would be the hallmark of His discipleship. This radical love, characterized by selflessness, compassion, and sacrificial giving, stands in stark contrast to the methods employed by worldly kingdoms.

Instead of seeking to coerce or dominate others, Jesus taught His followers to serve and uplift those in need, to extend grace and forgiveness to the marginalized and oppressed, and to embody the values of the Kingdom of Heaven in their daily lives. Through acts of kindness, compassion, and reconciliation, His disciples would bear witness to the transformative power of God's love, drawing others into the embrace of His Kingdom.

Through such actions, the Kingdom of Heaven expands through the Church, transcending boundaries to encompass cities, nations, and ultimately, the entire world. The goal is for the Kingdom of Heaven to expand until it reclaims the dominion and influence over the earth that was initially established by God in Genesis.

Central to this endeavor lies the divine triune nature of God—the Father, the Son, and the Holy Spirit—each playing a unique yet interconnected role in the establishment and expansion of the Kingdom of Heaven on earth.

At the pinnacle of this divine hierarchy sits the Father, sovereign ruler and King over all creation. His authority is absolute, His wisdom unfathomable, and His love boundless. It is He who sits upon the throne of heaven, orchestrating the unfolding of His redemptive plan with unerring precision and grace.

Seated at the right hand of the Father is Jesus Christ, the eternal Son and Savior of humanity. In His earthly ministry, Jesus embodied the very essence of the Kingdom of Heaven, proclaiming its arrival and demonstrating its transformative power through His words and deeds. Through His sacrificial death and resurrection, He secured victory over sin and death, paving the way for humanity's reconciliation with God.

Completing the divine triad is the Holy Spirit, the divine presence and power at work within the hearts of believers. Sent by the Father and the Son, the Holy Spirit serves as the agent of transformation, illuminating hearts and minds with the truth of God's Word, empowering believers to live lives of faithfulness and obedience, and uniting them in communion with God and one another.

Though distinct in their roles within the Trinity, the Father, the Son, and the Holy Spirit operate in perfect unity, each working harmoniously to fulfill the divine purposes of the Kingdom. It is through their collective ministry that the Kingdom of Heaven is established and expanded on earth, as hearts are transformed, lives are redeemed, and the world is reconciled to God.

At the beginning of Genesis, God intended for humanity to have dominion over the earth and serve as His Kingdom Leaders. However, with the fall of humanity, our direct connection to God was severed, leading us to pursue our own understanding of leadership. This pursuit became self-centered and focused on gaining power and control over others, deviating from God's original desire for Kingdom Leadership, which emphasizes focusing on Him and serving in His Kingdom.

Despite various people groups developing ideas around democracy, republics, and other government structures, God remains steadfast in His desire for us to live in His Kingdom. His intention is for His people to work together to advance the Kingdom of Heaven, as Kingdom Leaders, rather than focusing on personal desires for power and control. Throughout time, God has been unwavering in this desire.

Jesus' teachings on the Kingdom of Heaven reflect God's desire to reconnect with us on earth in a personal way, rather than being confined to the temple. The establishment of the Church through Christ's death allowed the Kingdom of Heaven to enter the earth. For the Church to succeed, Kingdom Leaders must identify how they can best support the original intent by enabling the Church to spread throughout the nations as Christians carry the Gospel and the Kingdom wherever they go.

True to His nature, God's plan and purpose for His Kingdom remain unchanged, as the Basileia of Genesis is synonymous with the Basileia of the Gospels. This continuity through time demonstrates that God's intentions and desires for His Kingdom are steadfast and eternal. It provides us with an understanding that God's plan will always come to fruition, even if it unfolds in ways and times beyond our comprehension. As we look at the continuity of Basileia in God's Kingdom from Genesis to the Gospels, we are reminded of His unwavering commitment to His creation and His eternal purpose to restore and redeem the world.

Reflecting on these concepts, we can discern how God originally intended for humanity to exercise Basileia over the earth. This approach is purposefully different from the human-developed ideas that emerged separate from God. God designed each of us with unique purposes to provide Kingdom Leadership and stewardship over the earth. For Kingdom Leaders to achieve this, establishing a connection with a Church is imperative to ensure mutual support.

From the above, a clear understanding can be obtained of how the Kingdom of Heaven is to expand through the Church and it is Kingdom Leaders to encompass all nations, ensuring that God's Kingdom exerts influence over the nations.

CHAPTER REFLECTION

Scriptures to Read

Matthew 28:18-20	Genesis 1:26-27	Genesis 2:5-7
Psalm 5:4	Habakkuk 1:13	Isaiah 64:8
Ephesians 1:4	Matthew 3:1-2	Luke 9:1-2
Matthew 25:34	Isaiah 40:3-4	Matthew 9:35

Key Concepts

- God desires us to live as Kingdom Leaders, serving and expanding His Kingdom's presence on earth.
- Humanity was created by God with purpose on earth, and He delegated His authority to us to have dominion.
- Due to sin, the connection between Earth and Heaven was broken. As a result, God sent Jesus to restore this connection.
- Through Jesus' death and resurrection, the power of sin was broken, the presence of God was released, the connection between Heaven and Earth was restored, and His Church was established.
- The Kingdom of Heaven will spread to all nations through the Church, serving as the conduit for its growth and influence across the world.
- Those who acknowledge Jesus as their Lord and Savior receive delegated Kingdom Leadership authority. They are called to serve through their talents, gifts, and abilities to expand the Kingdom.
- The biblical concept of "Basileia," meaning both Kingdom and Dominion, reflects God's intentional plan for humanity from creation to the present day.

CHAPTER TWO

APPLYING KINGDOM LEADERSHIP

DEVELOPING INTO A KINGDOM LEADER

With a new perspective on the origin of leadership, recognizing that God provided leadership authority to humanity for dominion over the earth, it is now essential to consider how to develop into the Kingdom Leaders God has called us to be. Merely understanding this concept will not enable Christians to become the Kingdom Leaders needed to advance the Kingdom of Heaven.

There must be a solid foundation upon which to build the Kingdom Leadership framework along with an understanding of one's individual purpose. This is imperative as it provides the platform on which to build Kingdom Leadership. How does an individual understand their purpose? By looking at the specific talents, gifts, and abilities God has placed within each person on earth.

Jesus calls all of us to go and preach the Gospel and spread the Kingdom of Heaven on earth. However, individuals cannot all do the same thing, as this would only reach a limited audience. To reach all of humanity, God has instilled in each of us specific talents, gifts, and abilities that only we can use to reach the people He intends for us to impact.

If an individual is not using the talents, gifts, and abilities given to them as a Kingdom Leader, they are not fulfilling the purpose God intended for them. This hinders the overall effectiveness of the Church and limits its ability to advance the Kingdom of Heaven.

WHAT IS KINGDOM LEADERSHIP?

To operate within the Kingdom of Heaven, an individual must first become a citizen of the Kingdom, just as every person on earth is a citizen or resident of a country. To become a leader within a nation, one must either be naturally born into it or take a pledge of allegiance upon reaching a certain age, committing to serve the nation's best interests. Similarly, to serve as a Kingdom Leader, one must commit to the Kingdom of Heaven.

To make a commitment to the Kingdom of Heaven, a person must acknowledge that:

- Jesus Christ was the Son of God on earth.
- Jesus died on the cross as the way of forgiveness of their sin and the salvation for humanity.
- Jesus rose again on the third day after death and is seated at the right hand of God.
- To follow Jesus, a disciple must surrender their own will and desires to God.

Upon acknowledging these four statements and accepting Christ as the Lord of their life, a person becomes a member of the Kingdom of Heaven. This process is similar to how nations require individuals to believe in certain core principles and make a declaration of allegiance. By joining the Kingdom of Heaven, an individual is now positioned to take on a Kingdom Leadership role.

As individuals become part of the Kingdom of Heaven and find a Church to connect with, there is much for them to learn and grow in. Elders of the Church must apply wisdom to identify how best to support these new citizens of the Kingdom. New Christians will need to learn new ways and concepts of living, leaving behind their old ways and embracing the way of Christ. Teaching new Christians about Scripture is a vital aspect of the Christian faith. Paul encouraged Timothy and continues to inspire Christians today about the profound impact Scripture can have on a person's life.

> "All scripture is breathed out by God and profitable for teaching, for reproof, for correction, and for training in righteousness." 2 Timothy 3:16

Through this process, new Christians will begin to seek their purpose and position within the Body of Christ. To aid in this process, support must be provided to help individuals identify their spiritual talents, gifts, and abilities, forming the foundation for their development into the Kingdom Leaders God has called them to be.

In this regard, many Christians who have been in the Church for years may not be fully aware of their spiritual giftings from God. They might feel connected to the Church but not actively engaged in meaningful ways. It is equally important for them to identify their purpose through their spiritual talents, gifts, and abilities to effectively support and advance their Church and the Kingdom of Heaven as Kingdom Leaders.

For every individual who is a citizen of the Kingdom of Heaven, being connected to a Church is crucial. Hebrews 10:24-25 urges all Christians to gather to encourage and support one another.

> *"And let us consider how to stir up one another to love and good works, not neglecting to meet together, as is the habit of some, but encouraging one another…."*

The Church represents the Body of Christ, and its success hinges on the active participation of all members. Just as a branch severed from the vine withers and dies, Christians who are not connected to the Church can stagnate spiritually. Moreover, lacking connection to a Church limits the impact one can have as a Kingdom Leader, as there is no supportive community for personal development and the potential influence is constrained.

Being a Kingdom Leader also means conducting ourselves with integrity, transparency, ethical conduct, humility, and compassion in all aspects of our lives. It involves treating our fellow Church members, colleagues and clients with dignity and respect, recognizing their inherent value as individuals. We should strive for excellence in all tasks, whether big or small, understanding that our work reflects our commitment to Kingdom principles.

By consistently demonstrating these qualities, we not only honor the Father but also serve as a testament to the transformative power of Kingdom Leadership. Our actions should inspire others to seek the same values, thereby positively impacting our communities and society.

Where does an individual begin, then, to identify their purpose as a Kingdom Leader once they are a citizen of the Kingdom? It begins with identifying their spiritual talents, gifts, and abilities.

ACTIONING KINGDOM LEADERSHIP

The path to unlocking your leadership potential begins with recognizing and embracing the unique talents, gifts, and abilities entrusted to you by God. It entails a journey of self-discovery, where you delve deep into your innermost being to unearth the treasures hidden within. By cultivating and honing these God-given attributes, you not only fulfill your own potential but also contribute to the greater good of humanity.

Indeed, the expansion of the Kingdom's influence across nations hinges on each person fulfilling their role and leveraging their unique talents, gifts, and abilities to lead. It is not merely about occupying positions of authority but about embodying leadership in every aspect of life. Whether it is in the workplace, community, or family, there are ample opportunities to exemplify Kingdom Leadership and contribute to its expansion.

Consider a small Bible group that meets regularly and is now planning a Christmas celebration. Each member of the group is tasked with a specific responsibility to ensure the event's success. Some members organize the food, others plan the gift-giving activity, some arrange Christmas games, and others handle the decorations. Even within this small group, each person acts as a Kingdom Leader, ensuring the success of their respective area.

There may be a person in the Church undergoing chemotherapy, which places a significant strain on their family, especially with preparing dinner for the children in the evenings. Church members, upon hearing about this situation, feel compelled to help. Even if they have never met the family, they step in, cook, and prepare meals to ease the burden. These gestures of kindness and support demonstrate their willingness to serve and care for their Church members. By using their culinary talents and their time, these individuals provide much-needed relief to the family, allowing them to focus on recovery and other pressing needs. In supporting the family, these individuals have lived out their Kingdom Leadership.

In a broader capacity for the local community, several individuals within a Church may feel called to bless public school teachers. They arrange morning tea for the teachers at a local high school, baking cakes, muffins, and various pastries. They set up the stall and provide the morning tea free of charge to the teachers, without preaching the Gospel or making public declarations. They simply show care and compassion to reflect Christ in that situation. These individuals are operating from a position of Kingdom Leadership, using their talents, gifts, and abilities to serve others and expand the Kingdom of Heaven.

During Easter, others within the Church ask fellow members to donate various chocolate items. They advertise for a couple of weeks, encouraging people to contribute. They then take the collected chocolates to the children's ward at a nearby hospital and distribute them to the children. No words are spoken, and no recognition is sought. They simply give to bless. These individuals are also Kingdom Leaders, expanding the Kingdom of Heaven into the world.

Some Church members may have had difficult lives, perhaps being raised in families involved in criminal activity or engaging in criminal behavior themselves. With a heart to help people in similar situations, they visit a nearby prison and start a ministry to encourage and uplift inmates, sharing that life does not have to remain the way it is. These individuals are Kingdom Leaders, expanding the Kingdom of Heaven.

Jesus reinforces these examples by affirming that actions done to others are also done to Him, as seen in His parable in Matthew 25.

> *"Then the King will say to those on his right, 'Come, you who are blessed by my Father, inherit the kingdom prepared for you from the foundation of the world. For I was hungry and you gave me food, I was thirsty and you gave me drink, I was a stranger and you welcomed me, I was naked and you clothed me, I was sick and you visited me, I was in prison and you came to me.' Then the righteous will answer him, saying, 'Lord, when did we see you hungry and feed you, or thirsty and give you drink? And when did we see you a stranger and welcome you, or naked and clothe you? And when did we see you sick or in prison and visit you?' And the King will answer them, 'Truly, I say to you, as you did it to one of the least of these my brothers, you did it to me.'" Matthew 25:34-40*

As Christians, this is the calling of Jesus to everyone: to examine our lives, recognize our talents, gifts, and abilities, and use them to advance the Kingdom. Whether contributing to a small Bible study group, supporting those in the community who are struggling, or reaching out to marginalized individuals, every act serves as an expression of Kingdom Leadership.

A few individuals cannot reach everyone, and as such, this responsibility cannot rest solely with the Pastor or Minister. Each person living out their purpose within the Body of Christ—the Church—is crucial. Therefore, it is essential for all members of the Church to actively engage in their roles as Kingdom Leaders to ensure the ongoing expansion of the Kingdom of Heaven.

By recognizing and embracing our specific callings to lead, we become catalysts for positive change and transformation. Whether it is in the workplace, community, or family, the collective efforts, guided by the Spirit and grounded in the principles of love, compassion, and service, have the power to expand the Kingdom's reign on earth. It is not just about fulfilling a duty; it is about participating in a divine mission to bring about God's purpose in the world.

The source of this leadership ability lies in the divine wisdom of God, who intricately crafted each individual with a unique blend of talents, gifts, and abilities. These inherent qualities are not random occurrences but deliberate endowments from a loving Creator, bestowed upon each person according to their purpose and potential. Indeed, the leadership an individual aspires to embody is not an external trait to be acquired but an intrinsic part of who they are.

God's wisdom surpasses human understanding, and His design for each person includes the capacity to lead in ways that align with His divine plan. He has equipped each individual with everything necessary to fulfill their calling, ensuring that no gift or talent lies dormant or unused. Every attribute given has been intentionally bestowed upon each person by a God who makes no mistakes.

In essence, the leadership you seek is not something to be acquired from external sources but a divine inheritance waiting to be realized within you. Embrace your innate gifts, trust in God's guidance, and step boldly into the role of a Kingdom Leader who reflects the wisdom and grace of the One who created you. It may take time to overcome past negative experiences that have made you feel less than the Kingdom Leader God has called you to be, but the more you step out of the boat, the more you will build your confidence in being a Kingdom Leader.

Indeed, if a talent, gift, or ability dwells within you, it signifies that God has imbued you with the potential to lead in that specific realm. As we traverse the landscape of leadership within the Kingdom of Heaven, it is crucial to continually reassess our priorities and maintain a central focus. Amidst the myriad of responsibilities and endeavors, one principle remains paramount: our unwavering devotion to the ultimate sovereign leader, God Himself.

In the pursuit of Kingdom Leadership, we must anchor ourselves in a deep and abiding relationship with God. He is not only the source of our abilities but also the guiding force behind our leadership journey. Our communion with Him provides the necessary strength, wisdom, and discernment to navigate the complexities of leadership with grace and humility.

By prioritizing our relationship with God above all else, we align our leadership endeavors with His divine will and purpose. Our actions, decisions, and interactions are infused with the love, compassion, and righteousness that emanate from His character. We become vessels through which His Kingdom is manifested on earth, reflecting His glory and advancing His sovereign reign.

Furthermore, focusing our leadership on God fosters a posture of dependence and surrender, acknowledging His lordship over every aspect of our lives. We relinquish the illusion of control and entrust our plans and aspirations to His providential care. In doing so, we experience a profound sense of liberation and empowerment, knowing that our leadership endeavors are upheld by His unwavering faithfulness and sovereignty.

In essence, the core of leadership within the Kingdom of Heaven revolves around a steadfast commitment to God as our supreme leader. As we orient our hearts and minds toward Him, we discover the true essence of leadership—a sacred journey of service, stewardship, and surrender that ultimately glorifies His name and furthers His Kingdom purposes.

As Paul wrote, each person needs to operate in their spiritual gifts to ensure that the Church can achieve what Jesus, the head of the Church, desires. Christians need to develop these spiritual gifts in their lives to operate as Kingdom Leaders and contribute to the Church's success in expanding the Kingdom.

> *"Now there are varieties of gifts, but the same Spirit; and there are varieties of service, but the same Lord; and there are varieties of activities, but it is the same God who empowers them all in everyone. To each is given the manifestation of the Spirit for the common good. For to one is given through the Spirit the utterance of wisdom, and to another the utterance of knowledge according to the same Spirit, to another faith by the same Spirit, to another gifts of healing by the one Spirit, to another the working of miracles, to another prophecy, to another the ability to distinguish between spirits, to another various kinds of tongues, to another the interpretation of tongues. All these are empowered by one and the same Spirit, who apportions to each one individually as he wills. For just as the body is one and has many members, and all the members of the body, though many, are one body, so it is with Christ. For in one Spirit we were all baptized into one body – Jews or Greeks, slaves or free – and all were made to drink of one Spirit. For the body does not consist of one member but of many. If the foot should say, 'Because I am not a hand, I do not belong to the body,' that would not make it any less a part of the body. And if the ear should say, 'Because I am not an eye, I do not belong to the body,' that would not make it any less a part of the body. If the whole body were an eye, where would be the sense of hearing? If the whole body were an ear, where would be the sense of smell? But as it is, God arranged the members in the body, each one of them, as he chose. If all were*

a single member, where would the body be? As it is, there are many parts, yet one body. The eye cannot say to the hand, 'I have no need of you,' nor again the head to the feet, 'I have no need of you.' On the contrary, the parts of the body that seem to be weaker are indispensable, and on those parts of the body we think less honorable we bestow the greater honor, and our unpresentable parts are treated with greater modesty, which our more presentable parts do not require. But God has so composed the body, giving greater honor to the part that lacked it, that there may be no division in the body, but that the members have the same care for one another. If one member suffers, all suffer together; if one member is honored, all rejoice together. Now you are the body of Christ and individually members of it. And God has appointed in the church first apostles, second prophets, third teachers, then miracles, then gifts of healing, helping, administrating, and various kinds of tongues. Are all apostles? Are all prophets? Are all teachers? Do all work miracles? Do all possess gifts of healing? Do all speak with tongues? Do all interpret? But earnestly desire the higher gifts...." 1 Corinthians 12:4-31

While delving into scripture might seem like a daunting task at times, the insights gleaned from Paul's writings are invaluable. They underscore the profound truth that every individual is called to a form of leadership, bestowed with talents, gifts, and abilities by the same Spirit. As integral members of the Body of Christ, embracing this form of leadership is not just a choice but a necessity to advance the Kingdom of Heaven.

If you find yourself grappling with a spiritual gift God has given you, such as the interpretation of tongues or struggling to articulate your prayers, do not hesitate to seek guidance from those more experienced in this aspect of spiritual practice. Surround yourself with mentors and Christian spiritual guides who can offer wisdom and support as you navigate your faith journey.

Moreover, if understanding scripture feels like a daunting task, do not despair. Reach out to spiritually mature individuals who can help unpack the richness and depth of God's Word. Engage in study groups, attend teachings, or seek out one-on-one mentoring relationships to deepen your understanding and application of biblical principles.

Conversely, if you possess talents, gifts, or abilities—whether they lie in speaking in tongues, discernment, teaching, leadership, or any other area—recognize them as blessings from God. Cultivate these gifts through intentional mentorship and training of younger faith Christians, allowing them to flourish for the glory of God and the edification of the Body of Christ.

In every aspect of your spiritual journey, seek out guidance, support, and mentorship from fellow believers. Embrace the communal nature of faith, leaning on the expertise and encouragement of others as you grow and mature in your relationship with God.

LEAD LIKE JESUS

How do we exercise this Kingdom Leadership? Through the serving of one another. Jesus taught that leadership in the Kingdom should be characterized by selfless service to others. He emphasized that true leaders should operate from a place of humility and grace toward those they lead, rather than seeking to wield power over them.

Plato advocated for leadership to be entrusted to the "best of men," enabling them to make decisions on behalf of the populace. Machiavelli espoused that leadership is attained through the exercise of power, instilling fear, and manipulation over people. He asserted that if individuals were harmed in the process, it was of little consequence. Carlyle believed that during crises, Great Men naturally emerged with an innate ability to lead and save the day. These exceptional individuals had unique qualities and leadership skills that set them apart, allowing them to recognize the needs of the moment, make decisive actions, and inspire others.

Weber proposed that transactional leadership, which involves using rewards or punishments to guide people, was a viable approach for a leader to adopt. Burns introduced the concept of Transformational Leadership, which involves influencing those around you to act and operate in a manner aligned with your objectives. Hersey and Blanchard formulated the situational model of leadership, which asserts that a leader must adopt a specific leadership style tailored to the characteristics of the followers they are leading.

Despite the thousands of years that separate these scholars, their concepts share a commonality. They all revolve around the idea of a single individual or key groups of individuals in positions of leadership and influence, guiding others toward their desired goals or beliefs.

The current state of leadership, as often observed in various spheres of human endeavor, does not align with the divine vision originally intended by God when He entrusted humanity with dominion over the earth. Rather than embodying the Kingdom Leadership model ordained by God, many contemporary approaches to leadership are marred by self-interest, exploitation, and a lack of stewardship.

In contemplating this dissonance, it becomes apparent that God did indeed provide humanity with a blueprint for leadership—a model rooted in principles of love, service, and stewardship. This divine leadership paradigm is illuminated through the timeless teachings of scripture, where God Himself serves as the ultimate exemplar of leadership excellence.

A powerful example of God demonstrating Kingdom servant leadership through Jesus is found in John 13:1-17, where Jesus humbly washes the feet of His disciples. Driven by His love for them, He took the time to sit at each disciple's feet, equipped with a bowl of water and a cloth, and personally washed the feet of every individual. This act of service extended to Judas Iscariot, whom Jesus knew would soon betray Him.

Jesus exemplified how to care for one another, including showing love to those we may instinctively feel do not deserve it. By humbling Himself to wash the feet of His disciples, He demonstrated that even as the Messiah, He was willing to serve in the most modest way. This act of service illustrates to the disciples, and to us today, that just as Jesus came to lead and serve, we are also called to follow His example and serve others in our leadership.

At the heart of this Kingdom Leadership model lies a profound sense of humility and sacrificial love. Instead of seeking dominance or self-glorification, true leaders are called to emulate the servant-hearted nature of Christ, who humbled Himself and laid down His life for the sake of others. This Kingdom Leadership ethos transcends mere authority and power, prioritizing the well-being and flourishing of those under one's care.

Analyzing Jesus' exchange with the mother of James and John offers valuable further insight into His perspective on leadership and its role within the Kingdom of Heaven.

> *"Then the mother of the sons of Zebedee came up to him with her sons, and kneeling before him she asked him for something. And he said to her, 'What do you want?' She said to him, 'Say that these two sons of mine are to sit, one at your right hand and one at your left, in your kingdom.' Jesus answered, 'You do not know what you are asking. Are you able to drink the cup*

> *that I am to drink?' They said to him, 'We are able.' He said to them, 'You will drink my cup, but to sit at my right hand and at my left is not mine to grant, but it is for those for whom it has been prepared by my Father.' And when the ten heard it they were indignant at the two brothers. But Jesus called them to him and said, 'You know that the rulers of the Gentiles lord it over them, and their great one's exercise authority over them. It shall not be so among you. But whoever would be great among you must be your servant, and whoever would be first among you must be your slave, even as the Son of Man came not to be served but to serve, and to give his life as a ransom for many."* Matthew 20:20-28

In this pivotal encounter, Jesus did not reproach the mother or dismiss the concept of leadership when she approached Him with her request for positions of authority for her sons, James and John. Instead, He seized the opportunity to impart a profound lesson on the essence of true leadership within the Kingdom of Heaven.

Jesus illuminated that genuine leadership is not about wielding power or seeking positions of prominence for personal gratification. Rather, it revolves around selfless service and sacrificial love. He exemplified this principle throughout His ministry, demonstrating humility and compassion in His interactions with others.

In this scripture, Jesus also addresses the indignation of the other disciples regarding the request made by the mother of James and John, for positions of authority and power. He does not condemn their desire for leadership; instead, He clarifies that such aspirations should stem from a place of service rather than a desire for control. This perspective shifts the focus away from ruling over others, as the Gentiles do, and encourages an emphasis on serving, just as He demonstrated throughout His life.

The wisdom imparted by Jesus resonates with the fundamental truth highlighted in 1 Corinthians 12, where the apostle Paul underscores the interconnectedness and interdependence of all members within the Body of Christ. Just as each part of the human body serves a unique function for the overall health and vitality of the organism, so too are believers called to serve one another for the collective success and flourishing of the Church.

In essence, Jesus' teachings challenge conventional notions of leadership, inviting us to embrace a paradigm shift from self-serving ambition to selfless devotion. By following His example and prioritizing service over status, we not only honor the foundational principles of the Kingdom of Heaven but also contribute to the advancement of God's redemptive purposes in the world.

Jesus' poignant observation regarding the manner, in which Gentile rulers exercise authority serves as a stark contrast to His own teachings on leadership within the Kingdom of Heaven. Throughout history, earthly kingdoms and empires have often operated on principles of domination and control. From the ancient realms of Babylon, Medo-Persia, and Greece to the formidable Roman Empire and beyond, rulers have wielded their power with an iron fist, imposing their will upon their subjects through fear and force.

In these earthly kingdoms, authority was synonymous with domination, and leadership was characterized by the assertion of one's superiority over others. Kings and emperors lorded their power over their subjects, enforcing obedience through coercion and oppression. The prevailing ethos was one of subjugation, where the weak were exploited and the marginalized were silenced.

However, Jesus presents a radical departure from this prevailing paradigm. He challenges the conventional understanding of leadership by flipping the script on its head. Jesus revolutionizes leadership within the Kingdom of God by rejecting hierarchical dominance in favor of humility, servanthood, and love.

By contrasting the prevailing norms of earthly kingdoms with the transformative principles of the Kingdom of Heaven, Jesus invites His followers to embody a radically different approach to leadership—one that reflects the very heart and character of God. In doing so, they become agents of change and vessels of grace in a world hungry for authentic, servant-hearted leadership.

From Plato in ancient Greece to Burns in modern times, and every scholar in between, their theories of leadership predominantly revolve around exerting control over others. Jesus unequivocally stated that this is not the model of leadership that should be followed.

Jesus confronts and dismantles the prevailing notion of leadership, elucidating that His paradigm revolves around servanthood rather than the exercise of authority for personal gain. He presents Himself as the ultimate exemplar of this transformative leadership ethos, urging His disciples to emulate His selfless example.

Jesus' authority, and consequently His leadership, transcended the physical locations He occupied, further highlighting His desire to serve others rather than seeking personal gain. In Matthew 8:5-13, we read of a Roman centurion who approached Jesus, asking Him to heal his servant. Moved by compassion, Jesus agrees to go and heal the centurion's servant.

The Roman centurion interjects, acknowledging that he is not worthy to have Jesus enter his home. Instead, he expresses his understanding of the authority and leadership structure within which Jesus operates, comparing it to the hierarchy of the Roman Army. The centurion recognizes that just as he can command his soldiers, Jesus has the authority to command within the spiritual realm, over sickness and death.

The Roman centurion's declaration of faith profoundly impressed Jesus, leading Him to comment that He had not seen such faith even in all of Israel. This story illustrates how Jesus' authority allowed Him to lead through serving others, revealing that He did not need to be within the vicinity of the individual to perform a great miracle for them.

It demonstrates that Jesus' desire to lead from the authority bestowed upon Him by the Father and to serve others was more significant than using that authority to exert control over them. It also illustrates that our authority and leadership are rooted in our faith in God, and we can only effectively lead and serve others when we acknowledge the source of our leadership and authority.

Jesus' ministry was marked by such acts of compassion, mercy, and selflessness. He healed the sick, comforted the broken-hearted, and uplifted the downtrodden. His interactions with people—from the marginalized to the powerful—reflected a profound humility and a genuine concern for their well-being.

In the ultimate expression of His Kingdom Leadership, Jesus willingly laid down His life on the cross, bearing the weight of humanity's sin and offering salvation to all who would believe. His sacrificial act of love epitomizes the essence of true leadership within the Kingdom of Heaven—a leadership characterized by selflessness, compassion, and grace.

By following Jesus' example of Kingdom Leadership, His disciples are called to prioritize the needs of others above their own. They are called to serve with humility, compassion, and love, mirroring the transformative power of the Gospel in their lives and communities.

Ultimately, the goal of this Kingdom Leadership is not personal accolades or recognition but the glorification of the King of the Kingdom. As

His followers embody the principles of Kingdom Leadership, they reflect the very heart and character of God, ushering in His Kingdom values of love, justice, and compassion here on earth.

LEADERSHIP FOR LIFE

The concept of leadership transcends the confines of organizational hierarchies, governmental positions, social privilege, or formal education. It extends far beyond the realms of power, privilege, and prestige. True leadership is not reserved for those who occupy lofty positions of authority or wield influence through conventional means. Rather, it is a calling that emanates from the depths of one's character and is manifested through selflessness, integrity, and compassion.

Contrary to popular belief, leadership is not about self-aggrandizement or the pursuit of personal gain at the expense of others. It is not about amassing wealth, accumulating accolades, or exerting control over others. Instead, true leadership is rooted in a genuine desire to serve and uplift those around us, to inspire positive change, and to make a meaningful difference in the lives of others.

Leadership is for all who are endeavoring to fulfill their purpose within the Kingdom of Heaven, serving others through their leadership. It encompasses every facet of life: in our families, workplaces, recreational pursuits, and churches. In 1 Peter 5:1-3 we read:

> *"So I exhort the elders among you, as a fellow elder and a witness of the sufferings of Christ, as well as a partaker in the glory that is going to be revealed: shepherd the flock of God that is among you, exercising oversight, not under compulsion, but willingly, as God would have you; not for shameful gain,*

but eagerly; not domineering over those in your charge, but being examples to the flock."

The use of "elder" by Peter at the beginning of this scripture is based on the noun form of the word, indicating it is a title for a person rather than an adjective describing someone's age. In this context, the noun "elder" refers to a person who holds authority by virtue of their experience and wisdom.

It pertains more to the maturity and wisdom of the elder rather than simply the length of time they have been a Christian. Peter's exhortation is directed toward those who have walked closely with Jesus Christ and have matured in their faith and wisdom, urging them to recognize their responsibilities as leaders within the Kingdom of Heaven.

He begins by emphasizing the importance of shepherding the flock of God that is among them. This entails caring for, guiding, and protecting those Christians who are less mature in their faith and relationship with the Father. To clarify, a younger Christian could refer to someone who accepted Jesus as their Lord and Savior many years ago and has been active within the Church for a decade but is still in the process of developing their faith. Conversely, a newer Christian might have recently accepted Jesus as their Lord and Savior, perhaps within the last few months.

The elders of the community must offer guidance and leadership to these newer Christians, helping to strengthen and encourage them in their journey of faith. They should offer oversight with attentive and responsible care to ensure that the younger Christians develop and flourish in their spiritual journey.

An elder should offer this willingly, motivated by the closeness and love they have cultivated in their own relationship with the Father. Guidance and support from elders must arise from genuine willingness rather than obligation or compulsion. Shepherding driven by obligation or compulsion can lead to resentment in the elder and create a feeling of insincerity in the care and guidance offered to the younger Christian.

Tying back to Jesus' teachings in Matthew 20, leadership should never be pursued for selfish gain; rather, as leaders our role is to serve those we lead. As leaders our aim should not be self-promotion or glorification but rather the advancement of the Kingdom of Heaven. In doing so, we encourage and support younger Christians as they mature and become active members of the Kingdom.

Leadership should never involve dominating others. True leadership is not about controlling other Christians to fit our preferences or agendas within the Church. This mirrors the fundamental essence of leadership as intended by God from the beginning, as depicted in Genesis, and aligns with the principles of the Kingdom of Heaven that Jesus preached about.

Peter's exhortation also emphasizes the importance of being examples to the flock. Being an example entails that every aspect of our lives, not just our words but also our actions and behavior, should reflect Christ, demonstrate love toward one another, and reveal our commitment to advancing the Kingdom of Heaven on earth.

Within this framework, leadership is not merely a role to assume. You cannot turn it on in public and then disregard it in private. Consider the failures of organizations and multinational companies, where leadership espoused certain values in public but engaged in embezzlement and misconduct in private, resulting in damage to the company and the lives of many individuals.

Consider politicians who publicly advocate for equity and fairness, making promises about what they will deliver, yet privately engage in corruption and manipulation for their own benefit, betraying the trust of the populace. Consider those who have publicly portrayed themselves as great men or women of faith, promoting Christ, but have privately failed in relationships they should not have entertained. If one aspires to be a leader, it must permeate every facet of one's life.

Leadership is not merely an action; it is a fundamental aspect of your being.

> *"Nothing is covered up that will not be revealed, or hidden that will not be known. Therefore, whatever you have said in the dark shall be heard in the light, and what you have whispered in private rooms shall be proclaimed on the housetops."* Luke 12:2-3

Since God knows the deepest workings of our hearts, there are no secrets between us and Him. He knows when we stumble, yet the good news is that He is always there to forgive us and encourage us to persevere. As we grow as leaders, we should view every opportunity that arises as a chance to serve others with our talents, gifts, and abilities.

To succeed as leaders, we must utilize the opportunities in private, when no one else is around, to hone and practice our leadership skills. The moments spent practicing leadership in private are just as crucial as those when we engage with our families, workplaces, and churches. The private moments, when there is no one around to witness the choices we make or the behaviors we exhibit, afford us the chance to integrate leadership into our very being, rather than it being a mere set of actions or a role that we perform.

Every one of us is a leader. We have been entrusted with the authority of leadership from God through Jesus Christ, who serves as the ultimate example for us to emulate. While we each have unique areas of leadership; collectively, we function as one body, working together to advance the Kingdom of Heaven.

Collaboration and unity are essential for our collective efforts to succeed. Through Kingdom Leadership, where we serve one another, the influence of the Kingdom of Heaven can permeate across nations until it becomes not merely a presence but the guiding principle behind how a nation operates. To achieve this, we must emulate Jesus' leadership example and serve others with our talents, gifts, and abilities. We must allow leadership to transcend being an action we perform and instead become an integral part of who we are, as we fulfill God's purpose through our lives.

CHAPTER REFLECTION

Scriptures to Read

2 Timothy 3:16	Hebrews 10:24-25	Matthew 25:34-40
1 Corinthians 12	John 13:1-17	Matthew 20:20-28
Matthew 8:5-13	1 Peter 5:1-3	Luke 12:2-3

Key Concepts

- Kingdom Leaders grow by understanding and utilizing their talents, gifts, and abilities.
- Kingdom Leadership is not something that can be acquired; it is a divine inheritance placed by God within each of us.
- Being active within a Church provides the ideal environment for a Kingdom Leader to develop their leadership skills, along with their talents, gifts, and abilities.
- Kingdom Leadership is crucial for its influence both within the Church and in the broader community.
- For the Church to successfully advance the Kingdom of Heaven, each Kingdom Leader must serve in a capacity that serves the Body of Christ.
- Jesus encourages His followers to seek leadership in their service of the Kingdom, with the right intent of selfless service.
- Kingdom Leadership is a lifestyle to live out, not just a role to play. It must permeate both our public and private lives.

CHAPTER THREE

RESTRUCTURING YOUR KINGDOM LEADERSHIP

ARE YOU A LEADER?

How do you view yourself in terms of leadership? Do you perceive yourself as a leader in your current circumstances? Alternatively, do you consider yourself more of a follower, susceptible to being swayed by the prevailing winds of circumstance?

Your behavior and interactions with those around you serve as indicators of your self-perception as a leader. By observing how you engage with others, handle challenges, and take initiative, you can gain insight into your leadership identity.

Engaging in Kingdom Leadership, as discussed in the previous chapter, is a significant step toward developing your leadership skills. This chapter will further aid you on this journey by providing additional insights and strategies to enhance your leadership capabilities. It will provide you with the mindset to establish the foundation of your leadership structure.

If you find yourself following others or expressing sentiments like "I am not a leader," this chapter will offer you an opportunity to gain insights into what you can do to shift your perspective and recognize your own potential as a leader. If you harbor the thoughts within your mind that you lack the qualities of a leader, it will serve as a foundational premise from which all other aspects of your life will unfold.

Our thoughts serve as the initial catalyst shaping our beliefs. How we perceive our capacity for leadership plays a pivotal role in determining our actions and potential within our role as a leader. Once our self-belief undergoes a transformation, it inherently extends to shaping our convictions, particularly regarding what we steadfastly hold as true within our mental framework. This pertains to our self-asserted truths about our capabilities and identity as a leader.

Convictions act as a catalyst in shaping our attitudes. Your attitude shifts according to the convictions you hold in your mind regarding how a leader should interact with those around them. Your attitude toward leadership is pivotal to change, as failure to control it can lead to your attitude taking control of you instead.

Attitude subsequently shapes perception. Once you have progressed through the preceding stages of your thoughts, beliefs, convictions, and attitudes, your perception of yourself in relation to God and the purpose He has designated for you in a leadership capacity will alter.

Inevitably, your behavior will transform as you begin to think of yourself differently, adopt new beliefs, form convictions about your identity, and engage with an attitude that mirrors these convictions; consequently, you will perceive your relationship with God in a new light.

As your behavior is a manifestation of internal constructs, and your actions mirror the essence of who you are internally, significant shifts will naturally occur as your convictions change. Ultimately, your behavior will be transformed.

In essence, your leadership journey commences with your thoughts of what it should or should not entail. These thoughts inevitably influence all facets of your life, but we will concentrate on their implications within the realm of leadership.

SHIFT YOUR THINKING - CHANGE YOUR BELIEFS

Prior to moving to Myanmar, I had previously held some minor management positions in Australia, but none that wielded significant influence over many individuals. I lacked formal training in any specific area, aside from completing my carpentry apprenticeship, and had never worked in an organization comprising more than perhaps 30 people.

Regardless, I possessed a seed planted during my teenage years—a thought that I was called by God to be a leader, capable of influencing those around me. I clung to this seed, nurturing it within my thoughts until, eventually, it became an inherent part of my identity.

I believed that I held some influence as a leader, a belief that started from a tiny thought. From there, regardless of the challenges presented, I harbored the confidence that I could overcome them, grounded in the understanding of the giftings God had instilled within me and the purpose He had bestowed upon me.

By the time I departed Myanmar, I had attained an influential position within a property development company, a role that left an impact on numerous individuals. I successfully obtained my Bachelor of Business in Finance had started progressing through my MBA program, with a discipline in leadership, providing me with formal training in the field. Throughout this period, I had the privilege of interacting with leaders from various international organizations and institutions.

Furthermore, I dedicated two years to serving as the Chairperson of an INGO, where I supervised peacebuilding projects in regions of Myanmar affected by conflict. These accomplishments stemmed from me thinking that I was a leader, called by God, and served as the foundation from which everything else was able to unfold.

God, through Paul, communicated His desire that we would not conform to the patterns of this world, including its ideologies and teachings on life and leadership. In Romans 12:2, it states:

> *"Do not be conformed to this world but be transformed by the renewal of your mind …."*

Further, in 2 Corinthians 10:5 we read:

> *"We destroy arguments and every lofty opinion raised against the knowledge of God and take every thought captive to obey Christ."*

Narratives constructed in the minds of individuals about identity hold considerable influence over the trajectory of the lives they live. Prominent figures outside the church have echoed similar sentiments. Their message emphasizes the profound impact that our self-perceptions and inner dialogue have on our actions and lifestyles. The Bible echoes this same truth in Proverbs 23:7,

> *"For as he thinketh in his heart, so is he …."* KJV

This concept is frequently quoted, yet its application in our lives is often overlooked or underutilized. In practice, aspiring to become a leader begins with your thought processes. Achieving this transformation necessitates a shift in your mindset, which begins when you consistently affirm to yourself that you are indeed a leader, through Christ who has called you into His Kingdom. This is the process of renewing your mind as Paul encouraged in Romans 12:2. Affirm your role as a leader by grounding it in the scriptures that speak about dominion, leadership, and the Kingdom of Heaven.

Even if your mind is not ready to fully accept it, reading about the authority and power Jesus has given you to live out Kingdom Leadership will help build the mindset needed to embrace your calling. God already knows and has placed leadership within you. Draw strength from this understanding as you reshape your thoughts to see yourself as the leader you are meant to be in Christ.

When doubts inevitably arise, attempting to undermine your sense of leadership, it is crucial, as Paul wrote, to seize those thoughts and subject them to the authority of Christ. Dismiss those doubts and instead focus on the purpose that He has ordained for you to fulfill.

Allocate time for yourself, whether it is in front of a mirror, in your car, or any other place of your choosing, to repeat these scriptures as often as needed. Focus your thoughts on seeing yourself as a leader, and vocalize it aloud, so you are renewing your mind through scripture, daily. By this consistent repetition of scripture, you will engrave the word of God into your heart and mind, helping you to not only think of yourself as a leader but also to internalize this belief.

We seldom apply the concept of belief from an introspective standpoint, particularly when it concerns our own lives. We often state our abilities or limitations as indisputable facts without considering the influence of belief on our potential. This assertion of fact, however, merely reflects what we currently believe about ourselves. When we begin to change our thinking, our beliefs undergo a transformation as well.

Will your beliefs undergo a transformation when you begin to envision yourself as a leader? Absolutely. As your beliefs evolve, you will come to believe in your ability to influence those around you and recognize your significance within your environment. Without believing in your own leadership significance, it becomes challenging to inspire significance in those around you.

What exerts the greatest influence on our present beliefs? It is undoubtedly our subconscious mind. From the moment we are born, every experience, interaction, and piece of information we encounter is stored in our subconscious. This vast repository of memories and messages continuously drives our actions and behaviors, often without our conscious awareness.

Over time, we have internalized numerous messages from various sources—family, friends, teachers, society, and media. Unfortunately, many of these messages can be negative or limiting, such as, "You are not worthy." "You are not a leader." "You will not be successful." These negative affirmations become deeply ingrained in our subconscious, shaping our self-perception and dictating the limits of our potential.

When these beliefs settle into our subconscious, they influence our actions by creating self-fulfilling prophecies. For example, if we subconsciously believe that we are not capable of leading, we may not take opportunities that require leadership, thus reinforcing the limiting belief. These deep-seated beliefs can act as barriers, preventing us from stepping into our full potential and fulfilling the roles we are called to embody.

This subconscious resistance can manifest as self-doubt, fear of failure, or a lack of confidence, all of which undermine our ability to lead effectively. Recognizing and addressing these limiting beliefs is crucial for unlocking our true potential and stepping into our roles as confident, capable leaders.

To transform our leadership potential, we must actively identify and challenge these subconscious beliefs. This involves recognizing the negative patterns, consciously affirming positive truths from scripture, and repeatedly renewing our mind to align with a more empowering and true self-concept. By doing so, we can reprogram our subconscious, enabling us to take actions that reflect our true capabilities as leaders.

Paul's emphasis on taking every thought captive, subjecting it to obedience, and renewing our minds daily is critical for Kingdom Leadership. By actively capturing and examining each thought, we can discern whether it aligns with the truth and purpose that God has set for us. This practice enables us to confront and replace the negative and limiting beliefs that the world imposes on our leadership potential. Instead, we lean on scriptures that affirm God's desire for our leadership roles in His Kingdom of Heaven.

Through consistent and deliberate mind renewal, we break free from the constraints of worldly understandings and step into the divine purpose that God has ordained for us as a Kingdom Leader. This allows us to lead with authenticity, grounded in faith and clarity of vision. Embracing this purpose-driven leadership not only transforms our own lives but also positively impacts those we lead and serve in the Kingdom.

SHIFT IN YOUR CONVICTIONS - CHANGE YOUR ATTITUDE

Once we have undergone a shift in our thoughts and subsequently in our beliefs, the next phase of transformation occurs within our convictions.

What are our convictions? I love what the Merriam-Webster online dictionary, under the "Kids Definition," defines conviction as:

2. the state of mind of a person who is sure that what he or she believes or says is true.

Paul addresses this process of transformation in Romans 12:2 and 2 Corinthians 10:5. Once we have diligently taken every thought captive and aligned it with the obedience of Christ, and consistently renewed our minds daily, our beliefs about ourselves undergo a transformation, leading to a shift in our convictions or state of mind. This transformation occurs within the depths of our subconscious mind.

When we commit to renewing our minds and beliefs daily, our subconscious undergoes a transformation that influences our state of mind, ultimately reshaping our convictions. We become so assured in our leadership capabilities that our beliefs and declarations in this regard become deeply ingrained truths to us.

Now, consider the opposite scenario. If we have harbored thoughts and beliefs for an extended period that we are not leaders, that we lack leadership qualities, that leadership is reserved for a select few or innate to certain individuals, that only those who wield power or seize it forcefully can be considered leaders, then ... leadership becomes contingent upon possessing a specific position, title, or status.

When we have entrenched these beliefs within ourselves for an extended period, they become our convictions. We become so certain of them that we readily affirm and vocalize that we are not leaders.

If we are to alter our convictions, it is essential to introduce new thoughts and beliefs into our mental diet, thereby initiating the change we desire. Continuously indulging in the narrative that the world has perpetuated for millennia will hinder us from attaining the leadership role God has destined for us to fulfill.

Our convictions wield significant influence over our lives as they directly shape the decisions we make. If we lack conviction in the truth, goodness, worthiness, or achievability of something, we are inclined to make decisions that steer clear of engaging with it. When we are firmly convinced and hold the conviction that we are leaders, this is what we readily believe and confidently proclaim.

This conviction directly influences our attitude. While "attitude" encompasses various definitions, let us examine one from the Merriam-Webster online dictionary.

4. a : a mental position with regard to a fact or state.
b : a feeling or emotion toward a fact or state.

It is intriguing how our convictions, our prevailing mindset regarding something we consider to be factual—such as our belief or assertion that we are a leader—directly shapes our attitude. Reflect on how we might have felt about ourselves and the attitudes we held, or may still hold, regarding leadership when we were convinced that we were not leaders.

We may have experienced feelings of despondency, emptiness, sadness, and a diminished sense of self-worth. These emotions may not have defined our entire life experience, but were likely manifestations of how we felt when we did not think, believe, or were convinced that we were leaders.

What changes occur in our attitude when we start to think, believe, and are convinced that we are indeed leaders?

Our attitude may shift to one characterized by feelings of hope, fulfillment, excitement, energy, and a heightened sense of self-worth. Our attitudes exert significant influence over our lives if we permit them to do so. Proverbs 16:32 states:

"Whoever is slow to anger is better than the mighty, and he who rules his spirit than he who takes a city."

God considers the ability to control our attitude, our spirit, as more potent than seizing control over an entire city.

As emotional beings, we experience deep feelings that can linger for extended durations. Reflect on moments when you have been hurt by someone—how long has that hurt persisted? Even recalling those memories now, what emotions and attitudes arise within you? Merely thinking back on past experiences can evoke these emotions and attitudes within us.

Reflect on something truly wondrous, an experience that filled you with joy and delight. Consider how warm and energized you now feel as you think about this positive memory. Notice how swiftly your emotions shift from one feeling to another and observe the corresponding change in attitude go from pain to joy.

Attitude holds immense power. It can exert significant control over us to the extent that if we fail to master our attitude, it will undoubtedly dominate and govern our actions and decisions. The impact of attitude on leadership is no exception. If our experiences with leadership have been predominantly negative, then whenever the topic arises, our attitude instinctively shifts to a negative stance, owing to the substantial influence it exerts on our lives.

Imagine the transformation in our attitude toward leadership if it shifted to one characterized by positivity. Picture viewing leadership as something inherently good within us. If we firmly believed in this positive perspective, holding it deeply within ourselves as an undeniable truth, and spoke about it with unwavering optimism, our attitude toward ourselves as leaders would undoubtedly shift from a negative stance to a positive one.

With this shift, we would find ourselves energized by leadership, as it becomes associated with a positive aspect of ourselves. The prospect of leadership would infuse excitement into our lives, as it becomes something we eagerly anticipate engaging with—both internally and externally, whether at work, at home, in school, at a sports club, across the arts, or anywhere else. Our attitude toward leadership would radiate positivity in every aspect of our lives.

SHIFT IN PERCEPTION - CHANGE OF BEHAVIOR

If we perceive ourselves as just followers and not leaders, others will also view us in that light. Conversely, if we see ourselves as leaders, others will do the same. Our self-perception is crucial as it influences how others perceive us. If we do not even perceive ourselves as leaders, no one else will consider us as such either.

Perception follows attitude. Our attitude shapes how we perceive the world around us. For instance, if you are having a particularly challenging day and your attitude reflects frustration, annoyance, disappointment, anger, or loneliness, your perception of your current life circumstances will likely be negative because of the feelings you are experiencing in that moment.

On the contrary, when life is going well and you feel joyous, excited, hopeful, energized, or loved, your perception of the world will be vastly different. This same principle applies to how we perceive our leadership roles and our interactions with those around us.

If your attitude exudes confidence and self-awareness regarding your identity as a leader, across various life environments, your perception of how you can influence and impact those environments will be one of significance and value.

When the driving force behind your leadership is rooted in service to others, those around you and your followers will recognize and appreciate the genuine value you bring. The philosophy of Kingdom Leadership, as modeled by Jesus, serves as a safeguard against arrogance and an inflated sense of importance, as it emphasizes leadership centered on others rather than oneself.

When you have a clear understanding and awareness of your self-worth, self-esteem, and self-concept, you will feel comfortable and confident in your behavior as a leader. These three aspects will be further discussed in the next section.

Behavior is shaped by your perception and is the outward manifestation of every preceding phase of change, leading to your current posture as a leader. One fundamental aspect of leadership is the inability to segregate your public leadership from your private life.

Leadership transcends mere actions or appearances; it is a holistic commitment to embodying certain values and principles in every facet of life. It is about being authentic and genuine, consistently demonstrating integrity, empathy, and accountability, both in public roles and private interactions.

Consider that many "world" leaders in various spheres such as government, business, and religious organizations have faced failure because they viewed leadership as a role confined to their public personas, neglecting its significance in their private lives.

> *"Beware of false prophets, who come to you in sheep's clothing but inwardly are ravenous wolves. You will recognize them by their fruits. Are grapes gathered from thornbushes or figs from thistles? So, every healthy tree bears good fruit, but the diseased*

tree bears bad fruit. A healthy tree cannot bear bad fruit, nor can a diseased tree bear good fruit. Every tree that does not bear good fruit is cut down and thrown into the fire. Thus, you will recognize them by their fruits." Matthew 7:15-20

Jesus placed significant emphasis on discerning individuals by their behavior, viewing that as indicative of their true character. This principle holds true across various spheres of life—be it within our families, workplaces, churches, governments, or broader communities. Leaders, especially, are judged by the behaviors they exhibit and the fruits they produce.

Leaders who produce nourishing fruit exemplify the transformative power of Kingdom values in action, fostering environments of trust, collaboration, and mutual respect. Through their behaviors, they inspire others to emulate the virtues of love, compassion, integrity, and service, creating ripple effects of positive change and impact within their spheres of influence.

Conversely, leaders motivated by self-interest often display behaviors that are marked by selfishness, dishonesty, and exploitation. Their actions are driven by a desire for personal gain and advancement, rather than a genuine concern for the well-being of those they lead. In contrast to the virtues upheld by Kingdom-minded leaders, these individuals prioritize their own interests above all else, often at the expense of others.

Jesus' teachings offer profound insights into the importance of discerning the motives and intentions behind individuals' actions. He emphasized the need to look beyond outward appearances and superficial gestures, and instead to focus on the motivations of the heart—the underlying attitudes that drive behavior. In doing so, we can distinguish authentic leaders—those who exemplify humility, integrity, and selflessness—from those whose leadership is marred by greed, deceit, and manipulation.

Leaders who prioritize personal ambition over serving others often exhibit a pattern of behavior characterized by a lack of transparency, accountability, and empathy. They may resort to manipulation, coercion, or deceit to achieve their goals, disregarding the well-being and dignity of those they lead in the process.

The behavior and fruit produced by leaders are indeed reflections of their perception of the world, which is influenced by their attitude. This attitude, in turn, is shaped by their convictions, which stem from their beliefs. Ultimately, it all begins with their thoughts. The effectiveness and influence of a leader can be gauged by evaluating their behavior and the outcomes they produce.

For us, when our thinking aligns with what God has called us to be, the ultimate result is the production of good fruit through our behavior. This manifestation of good fruit is not limited to our public lives but permeates into every aspect of our private lives as well.

Living leadership becomes a lifestyle choice, rooted in operating out of the purpose God has placed within us, rather than merely performing a role. It is about embodying leadership qualities in all that we do, consistently demonstrating integrity, compassion, and service to others, guided by our faith and devotion to God's will.

SELF-WORTH, SELF-ESTEEM, SELF-CONCEPT

Self-Worth

How do you perceive your value as a leader? Many of us tend to base our sense of worth on the opinions and judgments of others. As a result, rather than cultivating self-worth, we adopt the evaluations others place upon us. David wrote in Psalm 139:13-16:

> *"For you formed my inward parts; you knitted me together in my mother's womb. I praise you, for I am fearfully and wonderfully made. Wonderful are your works; my soul knows it very well. My frame was not hidden from you, when I was being made in secret, intricately woven in the depths of the earth. Your eyes saw my unformed substance; in your book were written, every one of them, the days that were formed for me, when as yet there was none of them."*

David recognized his self-worth and found it rooted in his relationship with God. He understood that God intricately formed him, viewing him as uniquely valuable. Even in the earliest stages of his existence, before he took physical form, David recognized his inherent worth as a creation of God.

Before any days were counted or time was spent on earth, David understood his worth, which was not contingent on external validation or earthly accomplishments. Reflecting on the account in Genesis, David comprehended the profound truth conveyed by Moses regarding the creation of humanity in the image of God.

The discovery of one's self-worth, rooted in the understanding of being created in the image of God, is a crucial aspect for leaders to explore and internalize. Self-worth is an intrinsic quality that originates from within oneself and cannot be derived from external sources. It is a deeply personal recognition and appreciation of one's own value, independent of external validation or approval.

God created each one of us to reflect His greatness and divine attributes, with leadership being an integral aspect of this divine design. As a leader, it is essential to walk in alignment with your purpose, which involves serving others in a manner that brings meaning and fulfillment to their lives. By doing so, you inspire others to discover their true self-worth and potential. However, it is challenging to inspire others in their self-worth if you lack confidence in your own value and worth.

By embodying self-worth, you create a positive and empowering environment that encourages others to recognize and embrace their own inherent value. Ultimately, self-worth derived from your relationship with the Father, serves as a foundation for effective leadership, enabling you to lead with authenticity, compassion, and purpose, while inspiring others to do the same.

Self-Esteem

When considering self-esteem, it is common to conflate this concept with self-worth. It is important to remember, that the foundation for your self-worth and self-esteem needs to come from what God has spoken about you in scripture. Self-worth centers on the value you attribute to yourself. Self-esteem pertains to the value you perceive yourself to have within your current environment.

Self-esteem encompasses the value you believe you contribute to various aspects of your life, such as work, school, church, or family. It offers insight into your perception of your role and significance in different contexts, providing a sense of your place in the world.

If we, as leaders, perceive ourselves to have low value in our environment, others are unlikely to view us as valuable leaders. It is crucial for us to have confidence in ourselves regarding the value we bring, as well as confidence in the talents, gifts, and abilities that God has bestowed upon us for a purpose. Each of us possesses unique talents, gifts, and abilities endowed by God, and it is incumbent upon us to persevere with these, as advised in the book of Hebrews 10:35-36:

> *"Therefore, do not throw away your confidence, which has a great reward. For you have need of endurance, so that when you have done the will of God you may receive what is promised."*

God has placed you here with purpose, not by accident, but by intentional design. He is not a God who acts without thought or plan; rather, He orchestrates every detail with purpose and intention. We must operate with confidence, knowing we have been endowed with talents, gifts, and abilities for leadership within the scope of our purpose, to serve and support those around us.

We frequently speak of God having a plan and purpose for our lives, yet we often timidly shrink away because we perceive ourselves as lacking value in the environments we inhabit. Yet, in the same breath we then quote:

> *"I can do all things through him who strengthens me."* Philippians 4:13

> *"So, we can confidently say, 'The lord is my helper; I will not fear; what can man do to me?'"* Hebrews 13:6

As leaders, it is imperative for us to recognize our value in the environments we inhabit and to draw upon the strength of God to operate in our talents, gifts, and abilities, serving others through leadership.

Self-Concept

How do you perceive yourself? When reflecting on your identity, how do you define yourself across physical, emotional, social, and spiritual dimensions? These thoughts exert a significant influence throughout the phases we have previously read, extending their impact to our attitudes. When God created us initially, He imbued us with His own nature.

> *"So, God created man in his own image, in the image of God he created him." Genesis 1:27*

We were fashioned in His image, reflecting His likeness. While this is commonly interpreted to refer solely to His physical form, it encompasses His nature as well. How could we express love if He had not created us in His image of love? How could we possess hope if He Himself did not embody hope? How could we assume leadership roles if He did not possess inherent leadership qualities Himself? Since God is love, we are capable of love. Since God is hope, we can possess hope. Since God embodies leadership, we can exercise leadership.

What are the implications of lacking this self-concept, this belief, in your identity as a child of God? The world is currently replete with individuals who strive to dominate others, resorting to abuse, manipulation, and oppression. They employ corruption and bribery to attain influence and control, resorting to coercion and force.

These are not attributes derived from God, but rather have become ingrained in many people's beliefs about what it takes for a leader to be successful. These notions do not align with the divine image of God.

God has granted us dominion over the earth, not over each other. However, even before entrusting us with this, He bestowed upon us something far more significant: His image. He instilled within us a reflection of Himself, depicting what He desired us to become. We must begin to perceive ourselves as leaders, developing a self-concept based on scripture. From this, believing in the image and nature of God in which we are made, rather than conforming to the world's constructed image of a leader.

Relevance to Leadership

Understanding the interplay between self-worth, self-esteem, and self-concept is essential for leaders to effectively fulfill their roles and make a positive impact on their environments.

Firstly, self-worth is foundational to leadership. It encompasses our sense of identity and the inherent value we possess as individuals. Without a solid foundation of self-worth, particularly as leaders, we may struggle to assert ourselves confidently and lead with conviction. When we recognize our worth and value as unique creations of God, we can embrace our leadership roles with confidence and authenticity.

Secondly, self-esteem plays a crucial role in how we perceive our contributions to those around us and the environments we inhabit. A healthy sense of self-esteem enables us to assess our abilities, strengths, and weaknesses realistically. It empowers us to recognize the value we bring to our teams, organizations, and communities, fostering a sense of pride and confidence in our leadership abilities.

Furthermore, self-esteem enables others to recognize and appreciate the leadership value we possess. When we exude confidence and self-assurance, others are more likely to trust and follow our leadership. Our positive self-esteem can inspire confidence and trust in those we lead, creating a positive and supportive leadership environment.

Finally, self-concept—the understanding of who we are and the image in which we are created—is crucial for effective leadership. When our self-concept is rooted in the understanding that we are created in the image of God, it transforms how we perceive ourselves and others. Instead of conforming to the image of the world around us, we align ourselves with the divine image from which we originate. This empowers us to lead with integrity, compassion, and purpose, reflecting the character of our Creator in all that we do.

As leaders, it is crucial for us to cultivate a deep understanding of our self-worth, self-esteem, and self-concept. This process of change starts with renewing our thoughts through reading scripture, which then leads to our behaviors aligning with our new understanding as leaders. When we recognize the value we possess as individuals, created in the image of God, we can lead with confidence, authenticity, and purpose, making a meaningful difference in the lives of those we lead and the world around us.

CHAPTER REFLECTION

Scriptures to Read

Romans 12:2	2 Corinthians 10:5	Proverbs 23:7 KJV
Proverbs 16:32	Matthew 7:15-20	Psalm 139:13-16
Hebrews 10:35-36	Philippians 4:13	Hebrews 13:6
Genesis 1:27		

Key Concepts

- Renew your mind daily, shifting your thoughts to affirm that you are the Kingdom Leader God has called you to be.
- As you renew your mind daily, the foundational belief of your identity as a Kingdom Leader will replace the years of false beliefs you previously held about yourself.
- The truth you now believe about your identity as a leader in God's Kingdom will become a conviction you hold onto, regardless of the challenges you face in life.
- Your attitude toward engaging in the Kingdom and becoming a leader will become strongly positive as you understand your purpose.
- Your perception of the world will shift as you start to see things in the bigger picture of God's Kingdom and recognize the critical role you play in its success.
- Both the Church and the broader community will notice a change in you, as these foundational beliefs transform your behavior to reflect this change.
- Build upon the foundation of God's word to understand the immense self-worth, self-esteem, and self-concept you bring as a Kingdom Leader.

CHAPTER FOUR

YOUR SEED AND PASSION

THE SEED WITHIN YOU

Are you of the opinion that you possess all the requisite skills within yourself to thrive as a leader? What would your reaction be if you were told that you already possess God-given skills within you to succeed as a leader, as well as in life beyond leadership, and that you simply need to nurture and develop them?

Over the last decade, smartphones have evolved rapidly since their introduction to the market, capable of performing a multitude of functions. In achieving this, the manufacturer meticulously integrated all necessary components into your smartphone to ensure its successful operation before releasing it into the market for sale.

The manufacturer also provided an instruction manual detailing the functionalities of the smartphone, outlining everything it can do. However, many of us may have never thoroughly read this manual. The manufacturer of the smartphone has asserted that it will be capable of making and receiving calls, browsing the web, sending and receiving emails and texts, playing games, watching movies, taking photos, composing music, and a myriad of other tasks. The smartphone possesses the capacity to perform all these tasks and more, yet many of its capabilities remain undiscovered by users who have not thoroughly perused the instruction manual.

Before releasing the current smartphone, the manufacturers meticulously test the phone's functionalities to ensure that it can perform the tasks they claim it can. This testing process involves subjecting the phone to various scenarios and conditions to verify its performance and reliability. They conduct extensive quality assurance tests to confirm that each feature works as intended and meets the standards set by the company.

Additionally, manufacturers may enlist the expertise of engineers, software developers, and other specialists to analyze the phone's performance and address any issues that arise during testing. Through this thorough testing process, manufacturers gain confidence in the phone's capabilities before releasing it to the market. They thoroughly assessed the phone's functions to confirm its alignment with design specifications and claims. What was the final step taken by the manufacturer before releasing the phone to the market, following performance testing?

They placed their image on it. By affixing their image on it, the manufacturer took responsibility for everything the phone could or could not do. Their confidence in the phone's performance was such that they even offered a warranty, promising to replace it if it failed to function as expected.

In scripture, it states God knew us even before our birth.

> "For you formed my inward parts; you knitted me together in my mother's womb. I praise you, for I am fearfully and wonderfully made. Wonderful are your works; my soul knows it very well." Psalm 139:13-14

> *"Before I formed you in the womb I knew you, and before you were born I consecrated you ...."* Jeremiah 1:5

When God crafted us in His image and formed each of us, He did so with full awareness of what He was instilling within us. The various talents, gifts, and abilities He intended for us to possess. He knew what we needed inside of us to be successful in achieving the purpose He has for us and placed it there from the beginning. After completing this, He imprinted His image upon us and situated us in this specific time and place for His purpose.

Let us consider mathematics. We often attribute our learning of math to school, but God instilled in each of us the ability to comprehend mathematics. It ultimately boils down to how we choose to engage with mathematics to nurture and enhance this skill. Some of us were encouraged in our mathematical abilities, while others were discouraged. Does that mean mathematics is inherent in some individuals and not in others? No.

The ability to do mathematics is already present; we just need to cultivate it. And what happens when we neglect to nurture it? We fail to improve, and as we repeatedly tell ourselves, "I am no good at math," we solidify this belief in our minds.

What convictions do we then hold about ourselves in relation to mathematics, and consequently, what attitudes do we adopt toward it? How do we perceive mathematics in our lives, and ultimately, what behaviors do we exhibit in relation to it? With all this knowledge and experience within us, what do we then impart to our children about mathematics? As mathematics is just one component of our lives, how do our beliefs about ourselves in other areas shape what we transmit to our children?

In Genesis chapter 1, we learn that God endowed all plants and animals with the capacity to reproduce and multiply, enabling them to populate the earth. Yet, for some reason, we often overlook the fact that God equipped us in the same way. He provided everything we need to thrive and succeed. We often find ourselves praying for qualities and abilities that God has already placed within us. God give me leadership ability. God give me love. God give me patience.

We should pray, thanking God for granting us love, and asking for opportunities to practice and develop it further. Thank you for patience; please grant me opportunities to practice and develop it further. Thank you for leadership; grant me opportunities to practice and develop it further.

God would not grant you a purpose without also providing the necessary tools for you to succeed in fulfilling that purpose. He desires your success and has provided everything necessary from the start to fulfill His purpose. Why? Because we are already complete in Him.

Likewise, the smartphone is fully equipped and prepared to fulfill its intended functions, symbolized by the manufacturer's placement of their image, on its release. When God created you, you were already complete and equipped with everything necessary to fulfill your purpose.

God stamped His image upon you—you are already endowed with all the abilities and attributes needed for success. Is it necessary to further develop those talents, gifts, and abilities to achieve success? Yes. You cannot develop though what does not already exist within you. We cannot acquire the capacity to breathe underwater or to roar like a lion through development. The only talents, gifts, and abilities we can develop are those that God has already placed within us.

It is time for us to begin practicing and operating within our purpose, and nurturing and refining these aspects of our lives, especially in our leadership capacity. This ensures that when we reach the finish line, we have fully fulfilled our intended purpose.

PASSION TO SUCCEED

True Kingdom Leadership is rooted in attitude and behavior rather than merely a position or title. It is about inspiring those around us, fostering growth, and serving others selflessly, rather than seeking to control or manipulate them. Individuals with an improper attitude toward their followers, and consequently toward the essence of leadership, might impose their will on others, yet they fail to influence through genuine inspiration. They assert control through the threat of violence.

What will set us apart in our Kingdom approach to inspiring influence, and what will fuel our influential drive?

Leadership influence needs to be driven by a deep passion for fulfilling your purpose. As we pursue God's intended purpose for our lives, we actively seek opportunities to utilize our talents, gifts, and abilities in fulfilling that purpose. Our conviction about God's calling for each of us plays a significant role in driving our actions and decisions.

Embedded in this understanding is our perception of ourselves as reflections of God's image and our confidence in the leadership qualities instilled within us by Him. Additionally, it reflects our sense of self-worth, self-esteem, and self-concept. Keep in mind that our convictions stem from our beliefs.

With this conviction, we start envisioning the outcome, the result of operating within our purpose, and begin laying the groundwork to reach this destination. When we have purpose, conviction, and vision aligned with God's plan, our passion ignites as a burning desire to do what is necessary to fulfill His purpose and run the race well, as Paul mentions in 2 Timothy 4:7.

Our attitude toward fulfilling our purpose shapes not only our actions but also how we interact with others. When we approach our purpose with humility, empathy, and a genuine desire to serve, our leadership becomes a beacon of inspiration. Instead of seeking to control or manipulate, we focus on uplifting and empowering those around us.

Collaboration and learning from others are essential components of our journey toward fulfilling our purpose. We recognize that no one achieves success alone, and we value the contributions and insights of those around us. By working together with a diverse range of individuals, we can leverage our collective strengths and expertise to make a greater impact.

Our journey toward fulfilling our purpose is intertwined with the journeys of others within the Kingdom of Heaven. Just as the various parts of the body work together in harmony to achieve a common goal, we too must collaborate and support one another to advance the Kingdom on earth.

Leadership within the Body of Christ involves a dynamic exchange of influence. While we may have a vision and purpose to guide us, we must also recognize the valuable insights, perspectives, and contributions of others within the body.

Remaining open to being influenced allows us to glean wisdom from others, learn from their experiences, and gain new insights that can enrich our own understanding and decision-making. It is a humble acknowledgment that we do not have all the answers, and that God can speak to us through the voices of those around us.

When we experience influence from others, it is essential to align it with the word of God to confirm that it is a positive, beneficial influence that supports our journey toward fulfilling God's purpose.

> *"Beloved, do not believe every spirit, but test the spirits to see whether they are from God." 1 John 4:1*

What role does passion play in shaping a leader's effectiveness? Passion propels individuals beyond mere preferences or hobbies, compelling them to fulfill their sense of duty and commitment to achieving their purpose. Passion ignites a sense of purpose that goes beyond mere interest or inclination. It is a deep-seated commitment that drives individuals to dedicate their time, energy, and resources to pursue their goals relentlessly.

When someone is passionate about something, they feel a profound sense of obligation to see it through, even if it means making sacrifices in other areas of their life. This level of dedication and determination sets passionate leaders apart, as they are willing to go above and beyond to achieve their vision and purpose and make a meaningful impact in their spheres of influence.

Leadership entails sharing inner passions and inspiring others to join in common goals. This fosters unity and collaboration toward a shared vision, inspiring others to follow. Passion-driven influence contrasts sharply with coercion or threats of consequences for non-compliance. It fosters genuine engagement and commitment, rather than mere compliance out of fear.

Leadership by force may compel followers to comply outwardly, but it fails to elicit wholehearted engagement or effort. Under such coercion, followers often develop feelings of resentment and frustration, impeding their capacity to offer the leader the support and commitment they desire.

Leading through passion entails a focus not on controlling others but on realizing the fulfillment of one's purpose-driven passion. Because this leader is not striving for control over others but rather yearning for the fulfillment of a passion, those around them are more inclined to engage wholeheartedly, motivated by their own volition. When followers have the freedom to choose whether to follow and actively engage with a leader's passion, those who opt to do so are more likely to commit fully to the endeavor.

When we seek to identify our purpose, we often turn our attention to various aspects of our lives, such as our career paths, roles within our families, or the pursuits we engage in through education or personal interests. We may believe that our purpose is somehow tied to these specific areas, expecting that by excelling in them or finding deep satisfaction, we will ultimately fulfill our purpose. Seeking God's guidance through prayer is a common practice when we are searching for our life's purpose. Many of us turn to God, asking for clarity and insight into the path He has designed for us.

Many people associate finding and fulfilling their purpose with achieving grandeur, fame, or wealth. This perspective often stems from societal influences that equate success with external measures such as wealth, status, or recognition. The ultimate purpose of our lives is to glorify God.

This overarching purpose encompasses everything we do, whether it is in our relationships, work, hobbies, or any other aspect of life. When we align our lives with God's purpose, we reflect His character, values, and love to the world around us, ultimately bringing glory to Him.

When our focus shifts from self-promotion to promoting and glorifying God, our actions and decisions take on a deeper significance. It becomes less about personal success or recognition and more about fulfilling our role as instruments of God's will and love in the world. This shift in perspective can bring clarity, purpose, and fulfillment to our lives as we seek to align ourselves with God's greater plan and purpose. In this we need to die to self as Paul wrote in Galatians 2:20,

> *"I have been crucified with Christ. It is no longer I who live, but Christ who lives in me."*

This contrasts sharply with the self-centered focus of the world, which we must consciously steer clear of. The world often teaches us to prioritize ourselves, seek personal gain, and self-promotion, regardless of the impact on others. Leading in this manner is exhausting and lacks genuine passion.

To lead effectively within our purpose and in alignment with the Kingdom of Heaven, we must relinquish our personal desires and prioritize seeking the Father and Jesus above all else in our lives. We need to earnestly seek and embrace the purpose that the Father and Jesus have ordained for our lives.

When we seek the Father and Jesus for a passionate relationship, our leadership will flow with passion, energizing us to persevere through any trials we may face. We will not seek to control or manipulate others; instead, we will aim to promote the Kingdom of Heaven on earth through the talents, gifts, and abilities God has given us. Operating from our purpose, we will have a passion to see His glory revealed.

Your purpose goes beyond your job, studies, or family. Your purpose is about leveraging your talents, gifts, and abilities to serve others within the spheres of influence you inhabit. When you are passionate about your purpose, you will not need to seek out followers or convince them to follow you.

Instead, followers will be drawn to you, either sent by God's guidance or willingly seeking your leadership. When individuals recognize shared talents, gifts, or abilities in a leader, they will be naturally drawn to learn more and potentially align themselves with that leader. Lead with authenticity and passion, and followers will naturally seek you out.

CHAPTER REFLECTION

Scriptures to Read

Psalm 139:13-14   Jeremiah 1:5   2 Timothy 4:7
1 John 4:1   Galatians 2:20

Key Concepts

- God placed everything necessary within the seeds of plants and animals for them to thrive and multiply on earth.
- God has already placed within you everything you need to succeed as a Kingdom Leader.
- Identify the talents, gifts, and abilities God has given you, and seek ways to develop them.
- As you seek God and His Kingdom, consider your talents, gifts, and abilities, and find a passion to serve with them.
- Leading with passion allows you to operate from a place of service and glorify God.
- Passionate leaders attract followers who seek them out, rather than needing to actively recruit followers.

CHAPTER FIVE

WORLD CONCEPTS OF LEADERSHIP

Comparing Kingdom Leadership with worldly concepts of leadership helps in understanding the diverse approaches and philosophies behind leading people. This comparison further illustrates the strengths and weaknesses of each leadership concept and reveals the potential cultural or motivational influences behind them. Most importantly, it highlights how biblical Kingdom Leadership significantly differs in its interactions with followers and the broader society.

We will delve into the philosophical insights dating back to antiquity, notably those articulated by Plato. Following this, we will analyze the thought-provoking concepts formulated by Machiavelli. Thomas Carlyle's leadership theory revolves around the concept that history is shaped by the actions of extraordinary leaders with innate qualities and exceptional abilities.

Moving forward, we will shift our focus to more recent times, exploring the perspectives of influential figures such as Burns, Weber, and Blanchard, whose contributions have significantly shaped our understanding of various leadership dynamics.

PLATO

Plato, whose life spanned from 428 BCE to 347 BCE, hailed from a privileged background, born into a wealthy Athenian family. Firmly rooted in his philosophical convictions, Plato advocated for the establishment of a Republic as the ideal form of governance for a state. Plato's philosophical views reflected the prevailing sentiments among Greek thinkers of his time, which stood in stark contrast to the expansive empires flourishing further east in Mesopotamia. Notably, the Babylonian and Medes-Persian empires, renowned for their centralized authority and imperial ambitions, espoused different principles of governance compared to the democratic ideals cherished by Greek philosophers.

In contemplating the role of leaders and their decision-making authority, Plato emphasized a principle wherein the ruling class's authority ought to be wielded for the leadership and betterment of society. Plato's belief system regarding leadership asserted that those possessing knowledge of what is inherently good should rightfully assume leadership roles. Conversely, individuals lacking an understanding of what constitutes good should not be entrusted with leadership responsibilities; rather, they should defer to those who possess such insight and guidance.

In Plato's philosophy, knowledge held a central and foundational role in comprehending the essence of goodness, thereby serving as the prerequisite for guiding and leading others. A lack of desire for leadership was also considered essential, as it was believed this would eliminate undesirable motivations from the leader.

Plato deemed four questions as paramount when contemplating leadership:

1. Do followers choose the best leaders?
2. Do leaders need to have special knowledge?
3. Do reluctant leaders make the best leaders?
4. Is it okay for leaders to lie to followers?

In addressing the initial query, Plato observed that as a society, it frequently fails to rally behind the most capable leaders. Instead, society at that time was often swayed by charisma or persuasive rhetoric, leading us to elect individuals who lack the capacity to make decisions for the collective good. Such leaders often prioritize the interests of a select few over the welfare of the broader populace. This tendency is particularly evident in leaders who prioritize the preservation of their own power and authority, rather than utilizing it to enhance the well-being of those under their governance.

Addressing the second question, Plato emphasized the necessity for leaders to possess knowledge derived from sources of intrinsic goodness, rather than merely adhering to popular opinion. However, goodness is subjective and often influenced by the leader's personal beliefs and perspectives, which may inadvertently prioritize the interests of a select few rather than the broader populace.

Plato asserted that in cases where rulers or leaders assumed their roles reluctantly, it was preferable for them to lack a personal desire for authority, and to instead accept leadership out of a sense of duty. According to Plato, this approach fostered a peaceful and harmonious leadership style. He thought that philosophers, devoid of any inherent craving for power, were best suited to lead, as their detachment would allow governance with a broader perspective and a greater sense of objectivity.

When a leader's primary goal in society during Plato's time becomes preserving their power and influence over people, it can lead them to prioritize maintaining their leadership position above making decisions that genuinely benefit the people they serve. This dynamic often influences their decision-making process, where self-preservation and retention of authority take precedence over the collective welfare of society. To maintain this position, Plato acknowledged the inevitability of lying by the leader, as it becomes necessary for the leader to ensure that the majority accepts their decisions as being in the best interest of society. This might entail misleading others during discussions about what constitutes goodness and persuading them to defer to their superior knowledge as the leader.

Reflecting on this concept of leadership in our contemporary world, it becomes evident that many individuals still regard Plato's leadership structure as a viable approach. In the current political landscape around the world, there exists a similarity in their structure where those within the political parties hold the authority to determine the nation's leader.

The populace does not directly elect the leader; rather, it is the party elites or influential figures who make this decision on behalf of the electorate. The notion of "I know best" and "you should all adhere to my beliefs" reverberates from numerous political organizations, irrespective of their size, echoing loudly from rooftops across the political spectrum.

In our contemporary society, where educated elites hold significant influence, the potential consequences of assigning leadership roles based solely on the philosophical beliefs propagated by professors and educational institutions become apparent. This approach can lead to harmful outcomes for families and children, as those with knowledge may impose their own perceptions of what is best for society. However, the concept of "good" varies widely across different cultures and individuals, lacking a singular, universally applicable definition.

In the context of reluctant leaders, why would society desire to follow someone who lacks the genuine desire to lead? Could their decisions then be driven by self-preservation, leading them to act in a manner that facilitates their removal from leadership positions? Considering these questions underscores the importance of leadership driven by genuine desire and commitment to societal progress. When individuals lack the inclination to lead, their priorities typically revolve around self-preservation rather than the collective welfare.

Consequently, their decision-making tends to prioritize personal safety or exit strategies from leadership roles, rather than initiatives that benefit society. Even if they persist in their positions over time, their reluctance to engage fully can hinder effective leadership. This reluctance often manifests in a lack of proactive efforts to advance their community or organization, resulting in missed opportunities for meaningful impact and growth.

Plato's leadership concept, rooted in knowledge and reluctance to lead, is undermined in that no individual can ever definitively discern what is good or not for another. The vast diversity of life experiences renders an individual's concept of "good" as flawed when compared to that of another. No amount of knowledge acquisition or self-awareness can grant an individual the ultimate insight to discern what constitutes the greater good and what decisions are right to make for the lives of others, whether in matters of state, government, business, or elsewhere.

The central focus derived from this concept revolves around the mechanisms of control and decision-making concerning the lives of others. What constitutes good or right for others, or at the very least, what aligns with the interests of the majority. Here lies the stark contrast between Plato's concept and the biblical leadership style.

While Plato's approach emphasizes controlling or managing the populace through reluctant leaders, the biblical leadership style centers on serving others. Plato's dominant ideology of "I know best" still prevails today, based on the idea that by convincing others to accept one's beliefs about what is good and right—while approaching from a position of reluctance—one can take on a leadership role.

NICCOLO MACHIAVELLI

Machiavelli, a native of Florence, lived from 1469 to 1527. He was renowned as both a scholar and a diplomat, but his fortunes took a downturn when the powerful Medici family ascended to dominance in Florence, leading to Machiavelli's loss of position in society. Machiavelli's insights into leadership, power dynamics, and other fundamental aspects of governance are encapsulated in his seminal work, "The Prince."

Through a series of pragmatic and often controversial reflections, "The Prince" explores the intricacies of statecraft, shedding light on the ruthless realities of political life and the tactics necessary for survival and success in the realm of power. Machiavelli's key question was:

Is it better to be feared or to be loved?

Machiavelli advocated the belief that instilling fear in others yields greater control and influence over their lives. Any means necessary to sustain fear, control, and thereby the power of leadership over an individual's life is deemed permissible according to Machiavelli's perspective. The rationale behind this assertion is rooted in the understanding that it is impossible to compel someone to love you, nor can one manufacture love where none exists. Instilling fear in a person is more straightforward, in Machiavelli's consideration because an individual's instinct for self-preservation triggers a response when they perceive a threat to their existence.

According to Machiavelli's leadership theory, the use of fear as a strategic tool ensures compliance and control within hierarchical structures. In this context, leaders who employ fear tactics establish a power dynamic where dissent or non-compliance is met with severe repercussions. Those outside this fear-driven cohort have little choice but to acquiesce to decisions made by fear-based leaders to avoid the punitive measures aimed at enforcing conformity.

In such scenarios, individuals find themselves navigating a landscape where the threat of consequences looms large, compelling them to align with the directives and objectives set forth by fear-driven leadership. This dynamic reinforces Machiavelli's perspective that effective leadership often hinges on the ability to instill fear, thereby securing obedience and maintaining stability within organizational or political structures. Consequently, those who do not subscribe to fear-based tactics may find themselves marginalized or coerced into compliance, underscoring the enduring influence of fear in Machiavelli's conception of leadership dynamics.

The concern with following Machiavelli's leadership style is that fear possesses tremendous power, and when allowed to run rampant, can inflict considerable damage on the mental well-being of individuals and societies alike. This phenomenon is observable not only within dictatorial regimes worldwide but also in businesses and organizations structured under similar authoritarian leadership models. Surprisingly, it can even manifest within democratic governments led by individuals who exhibit dictatorial tendencies.

The generation of fear can permeate a person's psyche without any direct external stimuli to that individual. Fear can be induced in individuals when they witness negative repercussions affecting others due to the actions of a leader. The utilization of fear holds immense power for those capable of instilling enough of it to influence the majority. We need only examine the utilization of fear during the COVID-19 pandemic, which propelled previously unknown individuals to positions of governmental influence.

Recent experiences during the pandemic have shed light on the effectiveness of fear-based leadership tactics, reminiscent of Machiavelli's strategies. However, such approaches raise questions about the essence of true leadership. Leaders who relied heavily on fear to enforce compliance may have achieved short-term obedience, but their methods often mirrored those of dictators rather than embodying the qualities of genuine leadership oriented toward the welfare of society.

In analyzing their behavior, it becomes evident that fear-driven leaders prioritize control and authority over fostering genuine consensus and collective well-being. By instilling fear, these leaders may suppress dissent and maintain order, but their actions risk alienating trust and undermining long-term cooperation. Such leadership dynamics, reminiscent of authoritarian regimes, highlight the ethical dilemmas and consequences of prioritizing power and control over ethical governance and the common good.

Therefore, while fear-based leadership tactics may achieve immediate results in crisis situations, their long-term implications for societal cohesion and ethical leadership practices remain contentious and warrant critical examination. Leaders who aspire to foster sustainable progress and unity within their communities must consider alternative approaches to that of Machiavelli's leadership concept, which prioritize transparency, inclusivity, and genuine engagement with the concerns and aspirations of those they lead.

THOMAS CARLYLE

Thomas Carlyle (1795-1881) was a Scottish philosopher and writer of the Victorian era, known for his works on history, politics, and social issues. He focused particularly on heroic leadership and the influence of remarkable individuals on the course of history. One of his major works, "On Heroes, Hero-Worship, and the Heroic in History" (1841), explores the role of heroic figures in shaping societies and civilizations.

In his book, Thomas Carlyle explores the concept of the Great Man Theory of leadership. His theory considers that exceptional leaders possess innate qualities, rather than skills acquired through training or education. These leaders are born with unique traits that enable and equip them to lead, thereby making a significant impact on society and history. The key tenets of the Great Man Theory are:

- Leaders possess natural leadership qualities from birth.
- Individuals inherently possess the ability to lead followers.
- Those in leadership roles are entitled to their positions.
- Great heroes emerge in times when heroism is needed.

The Great Man Theory of leadership suggests that exceptional leaders are distinguished by innate qualities that set them apart. According to this theory, leaders possess natural traits such as charisma, courage, and vision, which enable them to rise to positions of influence and authority. These qualities allow them to emerge during pivotal moments in history, when their attributes are most needed, especially in times of crisis, to inspire change or lead societies through challenges.

As the central idea of the Great Man Theory is that leaders are born with the essential qualities needed for leadership, Carlyle considers that traits and leadership skills cannot be taught or acquired through education or training. These innate abilities and characteristics are sufficient to elevate them to positions of authority, enabling them to influence and mobilize followers, drive societal change, and leave lasting legacies of their greatness.

The Great Man Theory, therefore, overlooks the significant role that a person's environment plays in shaping their leadership development. Early childhood experiences, both within the home and the broader community, help individuals refine and grow through experience. Factors such as family dynamics, parental influence, and socioeconomic background are crucial in shaping a person's values, decision-making abilities, and leadership style.

For example, a child raised in a nurturing and supportive environment is likely to develop empathy and collaborative skills, which are essential in leadership. Conversely, a child raised in an environment dominated by fear and punishment may develop leadership traits rooted in aggression and manipulation. These differences highlight the impact the childhood home can have on the development of a child.

Considering this, leadership development can be seen to be deeply intertwined with the values and influences a child receives from home and society. It cannot be solely based on innate abilities or traits a child is born with. Societal norms, beliefs, and ethical standards play a significant role in shaping a young person's understanding of what is expected from a leader. Qualities such as integrity, transparency, and social justice are key factors by which a leader's effectiveness may be judged. Leaders who align themselves closely with the prevailing societal values, whether good or bad, will be more likely to garner support in achieving their goals.

A comprehensive understanding of leadership must consider the dynamic relationship between leaders and the societies they function within. This challenges the Great Man Theory, which asserts that leadership qualities are purely innate and independent of cultural and societal influences.

Education, religious beliefs, and spiritual practices play a significant role in shaping a person's leadership capabilities. While formal education does not make someone a leader, it equips them with knowledge, skills, and critical thinking abilities that enhance their effectiveness in decision-making and problem-solving. Similarly, religious or spiritual beliefs do not inherently create leaders, but the moral and ethical guidance derived from these influences, can significantly shape their leadership approach.

The Great Man Theory is limited in focusing solely on a leader's innate qualities, overlooking the broader influences a person encounters at home and within society. Leadership development must go beyond inherent abilities, considering the educational and spiritual factors that shape a leader's growth. It is also essential to recognize that God has created each person with a unique purpose, and the talents, gifts, and abilities they possess point toward where they are called to lead with purpose.

COMPARISON OF HISTORICAL LEADERSHIP

Plato's leadership concept is based on merit and knowledge rather than wealth or birthright. Plato argues that leaders must prioritize the common good over personal interests and strive to create a just society where everyone contributes to the harmony and well-being of the whole.

Machiavelli's leadership concept advises rulers to maintain power and stability by any means necessary, including strategic deception, fear and force. Machiavelli underscores the importance of adaptability and decisive action, emphasizing political realism and the manipulation of power dynamics through fear to achieve governance goals.

Carlyle contends that leaders, distinguished by charisma and vision, arise during critical junctures to steer societies and imprint lasting legacies on history. He emphasizes the heroic attributes and profound influence of these figures, theorizing that their leadership abilities are inherent at birth rather than acquired through education or training.

As seen, there is conflict with these contending leadership concepts. Plato suggests that the common good over personal interests is critical, in stark contrast to Machiavelli who states that any action is permissible if it results in the desired outcome for the leader. In this Machiavelli asserts that the skills required to be a leader can be learned and implemented successfully by the leader to enforce their control, whereas Carlyle claims that leaders already have the leadership abilities they need from birth. This then differs from Plato's claim that birthright has no impact on a person's ability to lead.

The contradictions across these three concepts of leadership, highlight the failure of humanity to truly understand where leadership comes from, and the purpose of the leadership they operate in. Due to being derived from the construct of man's imagination, they all have failings in their ability to guide an individual into true leadership.

None of these concepts prioritize positive engagement for the followers, as they all entail a top-down approach to leadership that marginalizes the input and involvement of those being governed. In various societies across the world today, in various governments, institutions, and corporations, these models are reflected in various degrees of centralized leadership and limited engagement with followers.

It is astounding to think that even after two thousand four hundred years since Greek Antiquity, through the Renaissance Age, and into the Victorian era, humanity's understanding of leadership remains limited. Those who lack the "correct" understanding of what is deemed "good" are often marginalized, excluded, and even subjected to attack and ridicule. Individuals who are not born with innate leadership abilities are often regarded as inferior to those who possess these desired traits from birth. Other individuals have an insatiable hunger for retaining power, and often resort to attacking any opposing ideas or individuals that threaten their authority.

TRANSACTIONAL LEADERSHIP

Transactional Leadership, a concept pioneered by German sociologist Max Weber in 1947, remains a widely adopted leadership approach in business practices today. At the core of this leadership concept lies the straightforward premise that employees are rewarded for adhering to and successfully completing tasks assigned to them within the established framework of a workplace.

This encompasses both short-term and long-term objectives, with diligent oversight or supervision of employees as they work toward achieving these goals through task completion. Should an employee fail to fulfill their assigned tasks, they will face reprimand for their shortcomings.

Transactional leaders rely on organizations with robust structures and policies that empower them to enforce these guidelines onto employees, as well as to effectively manage and evaluate the work and tasks accomplished. In a transactional leadership framework, employees are not typically encouraged to exercise creativity or identify alternative methods for completing tasks, as doing so may entail operating outside the established boundaries and guidelines.

Within transactional leadership, hierarchy holds significance as it affords the leader control through their position or title within the organizational structure. They often exhibit rigidity toward changing processes and systems and tend to micromanage their employees. Because it operates on a reward-based system, transactional leadership often fosters limited personal connections between the leader and followers. This is because the leader must respond firmly should an employee fail in their tasks, a task made challenging if a personal relationship has developed.

TRANSFORMATIONAL LEADERSHIP

James Burns is credited with developing the concept of Transformational Leadership. In 1978, he posited that leaders and followers should collaborate to propel each other toward elevated levels of motivation and morale. The essence of the concept is that individuals undergo a transformation in their thinking, work approach, and interactions with others, enabling them to perform at a heightened level and deliver superior results on assigned tasks.

For transformational leaders to lead effectively, they must foster trust, admiration, loyalty, and respect within their followers. If followers fail to establish trust, admiration, loyalty, and respect for their leader, they may not perform to the best of their abilities, nor will they be willing to make the changes perceived as necessary by the leader. Essentially, the leader endeavors to shape the employee's thinking and behavior in alignment with what the leader deems appropriate and most effective for achieving the desired outcomes.

Given the nature of influence required in this style of leadership, a leader must possess certain personality traits and behaviors. Without these qualities, their ability to lead effectively within the Transformational Leadership Style may be limited. A transformational leader achieves success by leading change through personal example, articulating a compelling vision that inspires, and setting challenging goals that people are motivated to pursue.

If a transformational leader is unable to instigate this transformative change within people, they are unlikely to succeed in their leadership endeavors. Transformational leadership does indeed afford individual employees a degree of autonomy and creative freedom to enhance the way tasks are executed, thus enabling them to complete their assignments with a sense of ownership and independence.

The inherent challenge with Transformational Leadership lies in the assumption that the leader knows what is best and then seeks to impose their beliefs and concepts onto others, urging them to change to align more closely with their own ideals. This influence once again imposes a degree of control, where if the employee or follower fails to comply, they may face dismissal or consequences.

While growth and development are vital for every individual, true progress cannot be achieved solely through one person dictating what is best for another. A leader cannot fully comprehend all the talents, gifts, and abilities inherent within an individual. Attempting to alter a person without understanding their unique qualities can have detrimental effects on their well-being.

SITUATIONAL LEADERSHIP

The Hershey-Blanchard Situational Model, conceived in 1969, theorizes that there is no single model that serves as a perfect fit for leaders to adhere to. Rather than adhering to a fixed leadership style, the Hershey-Blanchard Situational Model suggests that a leader should adapt their approach based on the specific employee or follower they are engaging with. To accommodate this flexibility, managers needed to develop four key leadership capabilities to effectively engage with their employees.

The first capability, delegating, is characterized as a low-task, low-relationship form of leadership that is particularly effective when working with followers who can operate independently and require minimal supervision.

The second capability is the participating style, characterized by a low-task, high-relationship approach, wherein the manager collaborates closely with an individual who possesses high skill levels but lacks the confidence to complete tasks independently.

The third capability is the selling style, characterized by high-task, high-relationship engagement. This requires a leader to interact closely with followers who possess the confidence and ability to complete tasks but are initially unwilling to do so.

The fourth capability is the telling style, characterized by high-task, low-relationship engagement. In this approach, a leader provides clear directions to followers who require explicit guidance on task completion and ongoing supervision to ensure tasks are carried out effectively.

This constant need for leaders to adapt their leadership styles based on the type of follower they are engaging with can be quite burdensome. As a result, serious problems can arise between a leader and follower if the leader has misjudged the appropriate approach to engagement. A leader's integrity may also come under scrutiny if they are perceived to be showing favoritism toward certain individuals over others.

A leader may also appear shallow or inauthentic, as followers become uncertain about the leader's true values and principles. This model relies heavily on the leader's authority and control over the followers to ensure compliance with the varying leadership styles they are required to engage with, as well as ensuring they are employing the appropriate capability for each situation.

COMPARISON OF MODERN LEADERSHIP

As evident in these modern concepts of leadership, each possesses certain positive attributes, yet they all revolve around a common theme – establishing authority and influence over others to ensure the completion of tasks. These leadership concepts necessitate followers to adapt to align with the leader's vision of what they should be and how they should function.

In exploring these concepts, it becomes increasingly apparent that the leader's primary aim is to harness tangible results and optimize performance from individuals, often overshadowing the importance of fostering personal growth and development. Within this broader context, the leadership ideologies attributed to Plato, Machiavelli, Carlyle, Burns, Weber, and Hershey-Blanchard are reduced to mere managerial structures, primarily concerned with organizational control and efficiency rather than holistic leadership that nurtures individual potential and growth.

A manager's pivotal role revolves around ensuring that the strategic goals and objectives set forth by the organization are not just conceptual aspirations but tangible achievements. This involves adeptly orchestrating the utilization of available resources, be they human capital, financial assets, or operational infrastructure, to propel the organization toward its desired outcomes.

In this multifaceted capacity, managers are entrusted with a spectrum of responsibilities. They serve as leaders, guiding and inspiring their teams toward collective success. They set clear and achievable objectives, providing the necessary direction for individual and team efforts. Additionally, managers meticulously analyze performance metrics, identifying strengths, weaknesses, and areas for improvement to optimize productivity and efficiency.

Crucially, managers are decision-makers, tasked with navigating complex challenges and making informed choices that steer the organization toward success. They weigh risks and opportunities, drawing on their expertise and insights to chart the most advantageous course of action. Moreover, managers play a critical role in monitoring progress, continuously evaluating the alignment between actions and objectives, and recalibrating strategies as needed to ensure sustained momentum and adaptation to changing circumstances.

Embedded within the framework of these globally recognized leadership paradigms is a keen emphasis on effectively managing human capital. This entails overseeing and guiding the individuals comprising a team and steering the collective effort toward the attainment of predefined goals and objectives. Within this framework, an individual aspiring to lead from a position of authority ultimately finds themselves functioning more akin to a manager, tasked primarily with orchestrating the performance and productivity of their team members.

Reflecting on the concepts of leadership the world has promoted, it becomes apparent how their approach diverges from the Kingdom Leadership style promoted in the Bible. In contrast to the approaches discussed earlier in this book, which emphasizes exerting control and authority over others to achieve desired outcomes, the Kingdom Leadership model outlined in the Bible focuses on leveraging our talents, gifts, and abilities to guide and support others in their personal growth and development. This approach eschews the use of coercion or force, instead prioritizing the inspiration and motivation of individuals to willingly follow of their own volition.

In the contemporary world, Robert Greenleaf is accredited with developing the Servant Leadership model in 1970. This has been gaining prominence, yet there exists a distinction between his version, and the biblical

Kingdom Leadership approach. Within Greenleaf's Servant Leadership framework, the aim is to acquire influence over individuals through persuasion while concurrently serving them, thereby guiding them to complete tasks and work in a manner deemed appropriate by the leader.

This approach shifts the focus from serving through one's talents, gifts, and abilities to attempting to elicit a specific outcome from the follower that they may not freely choose otherwise. Greenleaf's Servant Leadership structure fails for another reason: it is perceived as a mere operational style rather than a leadership lifestyle, posing a significant challenge for leaders striving to uphold integrity.

True Kingdom Leadership emerges when it stems from genuine care and concern for those being led, inspiring them to willingly follow through the passion and love exhibited for where you find your talents, gifts, and abilities. Leadership achieved through alternative methods may yield desirable results, especially in business contexts, yet by broader definitions, these outcomes merely amount to effective management rather than genuine leadership.

Achieving desired outcomes within specified timeframes requires skillful management of resources, especially human resources. This involves assigning tasks, fostering productivity and collaboration, and addressing challenges promptly. Effective management ensures that teams perform optimally, enabling organizations to reach their goals efficiently.

Leadership prioritizes the development of followers rather than solely focusing on delivering outcomes. The true mark of effective leadership lies in empowering and nurturing individuals, so they grow and improve under the leader's guidance and later emerge as better versions of themselves, enriched by the experience. This enables Kingdom Leaders to serve more effectively within the Church and to further expand the Kingdom of Heaven.

CHAPTER REFLECTION

Key Concepts

- Plato suggests that leaders should possess extensive knowledge of life and society, prioritizing what is beneficial for the collective good. Leaders should be reluctant and not driven by a strong desire for power.
- Machiavelli argued that it is preferable for leaders to be feared rather than loved, asserting that those capable of seizing power by force have the right to lead.
- Carlyle viewed leaders as Great Men who naturally emerge due to their inherent abilities.
- Weber believed effective leaders could operate on a transactional basis, offering rewards or punishments based on followers' compliance with their desires.
- Burns emphasized Transformational Leadership, focusing on developing followers' abilities to perform required tasks.
- Hershey-Blanchard proposed that leaders should adapt their approach to each follower to achieve desired outcomes.
- These concepts center on controlling others to achieve desired results or goals.
- In contrast, Jesus taught that leadership involves selfless service to those around us, with the aim of expanding the Kingdom of Heaven.

CHAPTER SIX

FRUITS OF KINGDOM LEADERSHIP

TALENTS, GIFTS, AND ABILITIES OF LEADERSHIP

The first four chapters have played a pivotal role in questioning conventional beliefs about leadership and reshaping our comprehension of Kingdom Leadership. Chapter five enabled a comparison between the structure of Kingdom Leadership and those advocated by worldly standards. This reinterpretation of leadership has triggered a significant paradigm shift, prompting us to reassess our preconceptions and operational methods within leadership. This reimagining of leadership has essentially served as a reset button for our understanding, prompting reflection on our approaches and behaviors as leaders.

Similar to how a computer relies on an operating system to function according to its designed capabilities, we too operate based on an operating system crafted by God. When our understanding is skewed, when our thoughts and beliefs are misaligned from biblical truths, we cannot operate at the optimal rhythm intended by God. The Bible serves as our operations manual, and without daily reading, we may make decisions or take actions that deviate from God's intended purpose for us. It becomes imperative then to reset our operating system, in this to renew our mind daily, and acquire the correct understanding to fulfill our leadership roles in alignment with God's intentions.

The tangible manifestations of leadership, what we can observe in action, must also be cultivated in our lives. These outward expressions, the fruit of our leadership, reveal a visible distinction between the understanding that guides our leadership and the understanding they currently adhere to. It is essential to develop our character in alignment with Kingdom principles of leadership so others can recognize the inspired power operating within us, which is a strong contrast to other existing perspectives.

The outworking of our leadership serves as the initial point of engagement with non-Christians, who are drawn initially to our outward expression of leadership, long before asking into the understanding that guides our actions.

In 1 Corinthians 12, Paul emphasizes the diversity of spiritual gifts bestowed upon individuals, each intended to contribute to fulfilling God's will on earth. Those who prioritize seeking God and His Kingdom experience deeper engagement with the gifts of the Spirit compared to those who may recognize their gifting but fail to act upon it.

Individuals who recognize their talents, gifts, or abilities but fail to utilize them mirror the servant in Jesus' parable recounted in Matthew 25:14-30. Like this servant, they are aware of what they have been entrusted with by their Master yet have not sought to develop their gift, nor are they leveraging it to benefit others in the community. This could be due to their current mindset and self-perception. They might feel excluded or struggle with overbearing leadership and dominant personalities. Additionally, a reckless or lazy attitude might prevent an individual from seeking to expand their talents, gifts, or abilities.

In the parable, the servant returns the talent to their Master without any growth or impact. Even if the Master understood the reasons behind the servant holding back from developing and utilizing their talents, there would still be a measure of disappointment because the Master intended for those talents, gifts, and abilities to be used to their full potential. God created the Church to be the mechanism through which individuals, who may be held back by their current mindset, self-perception, feelings of exclusion, or struggles with overbearing leadership and dominant personalities, receive the support they need to overcome these challenges and operate fully from their talents, gifts, and abilities.

This concept resonates deeply with our journey alongside the Father. He intimately knew us even as He intricately formed us in our mother's womb, as beautifully expressed in Psalm 139:13. Only He comprehends the vast array of talents, gifts, and abilities He has carefully instilled within us. Not even our closest relatives or friends can fully fathom the depth of what God has deposited within us. When we navigate through life with the awareness, even if it is subconscious, that there exists something divine within us waiting to be cultivated and nurtured by our hands, yet we choose inertia, we mirror the servant in the parable above, squandering the precious gifts entrusted to us by God.

The Father does not desire us to remain stagnant; He calls us to action, urging us to utilize the talents, gifts, and abilities He has bestowed upon us. When we heed this call and actively engage with what God has placed within us, we emulate the faithful servants depicted in the parable of Matthew 25:14-30. By diligently nurturing and developing the gifts entrusted to us, we not only multiply them but also exceed their original measure. This faithfulness in small matters earns us even greater opportunities from the Father, enabling us to expand and stretch ourselves further in His service.

Leadership operates in a similar manner from within us. If we passively allow what the Father has placed within us to lie dormant and go to waste, we resemble the servant who failed to act upon his entrusted talent. Consequently, the followers whom the Father intends for us to influence and lead miss out on valuable experiences, hindering both our own growth and the expansion of the Kingdom of Heaven here on earth. It is through the active stewardship of our leadership gifts that we catalyze growth, impact lives, and advance the divine purpose of establishing God's reign on earth.

God's promise assures that His purpose will ultimately prevail, even if we fail to act upon our purpose and utilize our talents, gifts, and abilities in the present. This parallels the outcome in the parable where the talent entrusted to the unproductive servant is taken away and given to another. It is disheartening to consider the potential delay in fulfilling God's purpose for future generations due to our reluctance to step into leadership and steward our gifts effectively. By embracing our call to leadership and actively engaging with the talents bestowed upon us, we play a crucial role in advancing God's Kingdom and ensuring that His purpose continues to unfold for generations to come.

In the context of Kingdom Leadership, it is vital to understand that leveraging our talents, gifts, and abilities is not solely for personal advancement or recognition. As emphasized throughout this book, Kingdom Leadership entails utilizing these resources to advance the Kingdom of Heaven and to lead others by serving them. This means guiding individuals in areas where they may have weaknesses but where you possess strengths, facilitating their growth and development. By leading with a servant's heart, we empower others to operate from a place of their own giftedness and talent, ensuring that the legacy of effective leadership continues beyond our own influence.

Leadership within the Church is essential, and while certain individuals may hold specific titles or roles crucial for its operation, the responsibility for the Church's functioning extends to all of us. Each member bears a responsibility to serve within the Church, utilizing their talents, gifts, and abilities. This collective effort is vital for the expansion of the Kingdom of Heaven, ultimately leading to a greater influence within society. As we actively engage in serving within the Church, we contribute to its growth and impact, aspiring for it to become the prevailing cultural influence in society.

Considering that the Church embodies the collective Body of Christ, as outlined in 1 Corinthians 12:12-27, it is crucial to recognize that we, as a unified community, constitute the Church. The Church is not confined to a physical structure but rather comprises of the people who come together in fellowship. Therefore, utilizing our talents, gifts, and abilities within the Church to advance the Kingdom of Heaven extends beyond the walls of a building. This service can take the form of visiting those in need and offering comfort and support to those experiencing pain or distress.

Even if individuals do not attend church, we can bring the Church to them within the comfort of their homes. Our outreach is not limited to fellow Christians; rather, it extends to all. It is equally impactful when we utilize our talents, gifts, and abilities to serve those who are not acquainted with Christ.

Our actions play a powerful role in promoting the Kingdom of Heaven, as they often speak louder than words. While sharing the gospel verbally is essential, our words will lack impact if not supported by actions that reflect their truth. It is through our distinct actions that those outside the Kingdom will recognize the truth within us, creating opportunities for their hearts to open and receive the good news when we then share.

Our actions are the true ambassadors of God's love and the promotion of His Kingdom. We do not require eloquent speeches or charismatic presentations; rather, a humble willingness to serve suffices. How can we exemplify Kingdom Leadership, advance the Kingdom of Heaven, and spread the Gospel?

"Be kind to one another, tender-hearted, forgiving one another, as God in Christ forgave you." Ephesians 4:32

"Little children, let us not love in word or talk but in deed and in truth." 1 John 3:18

"Therefore encourage one another and build one another up, just as you are doing." 1 Thessalonians 5:11

"Blessed are the peacemakers, for they shall be called sons of God." Matthew 5:9

These examples illustrate how we can embody Kingdom Leadership, not only within the Church but also in our interactions with those outside of it. Through these actions, individuals beyond the Church can perceive a distinctiveness in our approach and the type of leadership we offer one another. This difference is also noticeable to the younger generation within the Church, shaping their understanding of leadership and inspiring them to follow suit.

The Church relies on us to lead with our talents, gifts, and abilities, fostering growth and mutual support among its members. It is essential for us to play a role in mentoring and training the next generation of believers. Beyond the Church, the wider community also benefits from our leadership in leveraging our unique talents, gifts, and abilities. Through our example, they can discern the difference between the world's standards of leadership and the transformative way the Kingdom Leadership principles have shaped how we live our lives.

This goes beyond the roles many worldly leaders play; Kingdom Leaders are demonstrating a way of life. Our behavior within society becomes crucial, especially as Kingdom Leaders, because it will influence how the world perceives the Kingdom. Our actions will reflect the genuineness of our relationship with the Father, either positively or negatively.

Leaders who operate from their talents, gifts, and abilities wield considerable influence over those who choose to follow them. These leaders embody their gifts as an integral part of their life, not merely as a role to fulfill. In the broader community, these leaders extend the reach of the Kingdom by exemplifying a leadership style rooted in service rather than control. Through their actions, they magnify God's goodness and glory, inspiring others to do the same.

CREATIVITY

In Genesis 1:27, God's act of creating humanity in His image, along with the entirety of creation as depicted in the additional verses of Genesis 1, showcases His innate creative essence. It is God who orchestrates the breathtaking beauty of the sky and sets the planets into motion. Isaiah offers a remarkable portrayal of God's creativity, expressing how He is:

> *"But now, O Lord, you are our Father; we are the clay, and you are our potter; we are all the work of your hand." Isaiah 64:8*

In Psalm 139:14, the psalmist sings praises to God, acknowledging the marvelous creativity inherent in His design, saying,

> *"I praise you, for I am fearfully and wonderfully made. Wonderful are your works; my soul knows it very well."*

God, by His very nature, embodies boundless creativity, evident in the intricate tapestry of the universe He has fashioned. As beings created in His image, we too bear the imprint of His creativity. In crafting each of us, God has done so with meticulous care and precision, leaving no detail overlooked. Far from haphazard, our design reflects His intentional craftsmanship, with every facet of our being serving a purpose in His grand design.

Indeed, there are no mistakes in God's creation; He has endowed each of us with a unique blend of talents, gifts, and abilities perfectly suited to fulfill His divine purpose. From the depths of our souls to the intricacies of our physical form, we are fearfully and wonderfully made, with every aspect of our being intricately woven together by the Master Creator.

As Kingdom Leaders, our expression of creativity extends beyond conventional perceptions or societal norms, encompassing various forms such as music or the arts. Some individuals are uniquely gifted in these areas, positioned to lead and inspire others through their creative endeavors. This leadership may manifest in guiding and supporting those who may not excel in these realms, or in nurturing and developing the talents of others seeking growth.

Exodus 35:35 beautifully illustrates the diverse creative talents bestowed upon individuals, reflecting different facets of God's own creativity. This scripture highlights the significance of artistic expression as a means of glorifying God and enriching the community.

Creativity transcends the confines of traditional arts and music. In Exodus 31:3-5, we find encouragement for creativity in working with metals and timbers. This craftsmanship empowers individuals to envision and construct stunning structures, offering glory to God through their skilled workmanship. Whether it is in architecture, woodworking, or metalworking, each act of creative expression reflects the beauty and ingenuity of God's design, glorifying Him through tangible creations.

Consider our daily routines and work environments. How can we infuse creativity into our workplaces to demonstrate leadership and inspire those around us? Proverbs 22:29 declares,

> *"Do you see a man skillful in his works? He will stand before kings; he will not stand before obscure men."*

When we innovate and devise fresh strategies to enhance our workflow or implement systems that yield superior results for our employer, our efforts will be recognized. We do not necessarily need to possess what the world considers as creative talents, gifts, or abilities to function as Kingdom Leaders. Instead, we must operate from our sense of purpose within our workplaces, embodying Kingdom Leadership principles and seeking opportunities to contribute positively. This involves identifying the talents, gifts, and abilities that God has bestowed upon us and employing them creatively to lead and serve those around us.

We should not keep our creativity to ourselves; rather, we should harness it to generate innovative ways to advance God's message and extend His Kingdom here on earth. Peter emphasizes the importance of maintaining this focus in 1 Peter 4:10, where he encourages us to employ our gifts to serve others, faithfully stewarding God's grace in its various forms.

> *"As each has received a gift, use it to serve one another, as good stewards of God's varied grace."*

When we step out in using our talents, gifts, and abilities as Kingdom Leaders, honoring God becomes paramount. It is essential to operate from a position of God's grace, acknowledging that He initially bestowed those talents, gifts, and abilities upon us when He created us. However, as we utilize these gifts, it is crucial to employ them in a manner that facilitates service to one another. This underscores the essence of Kingdom

Leadership—placing importance on serving others while faithfully stewarding the talents, gifts, and abilities entrusted to us by God.

As leaders, we leverage our creativity to innovate, devise, plan, or enhance various aspects in a manner that prioritizes serving the Kingdom of Heaven and supporting those around us. Whether as Kingdom Leaders guiding individuals who lack a particular strength in a gifting or as mentors guiding the new generation with similar talents, gifts, or abilities, our goal remains the same: to use our creativity to promote the Kingdom of Heaven and serve others.

TIME MANAGEMENT

Our time on this earth is finite, a reality we must acknowledge. Unlike God, who transcends time, we are bound by its constraints during our earthly existence. In Psalm 39:4, we are reminded of the brevity of our time on earth.

> *"O Lord, make me know my end and what is the measure of my days; let me know how fleeting I am."*

Indeed, the realization of our finite time on earth may be unsettling for some. However, as Kingdom Leaders, it should serve as a powerful motivator to pursue God's purposes with urgency and diligence. We cannot afford to passively wait or hope for circumstances to improve on their own. Likewise, we cannot rely solely on others to advance the Kingdom of Heaven. Instead, we must take decisive action now, seizing every opportunity to contribute to God's work and make a meaningful impact in the world.

As Kingdom Leaders, managing our time wisely is crucial to ensure that we make the most of each day. It all begins with identifying the talents, gifts, and abilities that God has entrusted to us. By discerning our unique strengths and abilities, we can align ourselves with God's purpose and will for our lives. Paul provides encouragement in this regard in his letter to the Ephesians.

> *"Look carefully then how you walk, not as unwise but as wise, making the best use of the time, because the days are evil. Therefore, do not be foolish, but understand what the will of the Lord is." Ephesians 5:15-17*

To truly fulfill our roles as Kingdom Leaders, we must earnestly seek out God's purpose and will for our lives. It is imperative that we walk circumspectly, making the most of our time and opportunities, as Paul advises in Ephesians. As Kingdom Leaders, our ultimate focus should be on promoting the Kingdom of Heaven. While we may find ourselves engaged in various tasks throughout the day, everything we do should ultimately serve this higher purpose. Whether it is guiding and supporting others, teaching and mentoring, or engaging in acts of service and compassion, our aim should always be to advance the Kingdom of Heaven and bring glory to God in all that we do.

Keeping our focus on promoting the Kingdom of Heaven amidst the distractions of the world is undoubtedly challenging. It is easy to become consumed by the tangible realities we see around us, leading us astray from our higher calling. The Corinthians, too, struggled with this tendency to fixate on the visible rather than the unseen. Paul addressed this struggle in his letter to the Corinthians, specifically in 2 Corinthians 4:18, where he urged them to fix their gaze on the unseen, eternal realities rather than being consumed by the transient concerns of the world.

> *"…look not to the things that are seen but to the things that are unseen. For the things that are seen are transient, but the things that are unseen are eternal."*

As Kingdom Leaders, it is essential to manage our time wisely, ensuring that the work we engage in aligns with the promotion of unseen, eternal realities—particularly the advancement of the Kingdom of Heaven and the service of others. We must guard against becoming entangled or burdened by the fleeting concerns of the world, prioritizing our efforts toward endeavors that have lasting significance and eternal impact.

While it is necessary for us to engage in employment to meet our material needs and contribute to society, we can elevate our work to a higher purpose by embodying Kingdom Leadership principles. In our daily workplaces, we can bring the values and ideals of the Kingdom of Heaven to the forefront of everything we do. This means conducting ourselves with integrity, humility, and compassion, treating our colleagues and clients with dignity and respect, and striving for excellence in all tasks. Prioritizing the Kingdom of Heaven in our daily work is of utmost importance, as emphasized in Colossians 4:5, where we are encouraged to conduct ourselves wisely toward outsiders, making the most of every opportunity.

> *"Walk in wisdom toward outsiders, making the best use of the time."*

Kingdom Leadership necessitates a careful stewardship of time. Understanding the fleeting nature of our earthly existence and the paramount importance of advancing the Kingdom of Heaven, we are compelled to act with purpose and urgency. This awareness serves as a powerful motivator, prompting us to diligently pursue God's will for our lives and make the most of every opportunity. As we navigate the complexities of our daily lives and engage with the world around us, we are called to maintain a steadfast focus on eternal truths and unseen realities.

This requires a deliberate effort to prioritize spiritual growth, cultivate a deeper intimacy with God, and align our actions with His divine purposes.

While we are actively involved in our workplaces and various endeavors, we must remain vigilant, ensuring that our pursuits are ultimately directed toward the glorification of God and the advancement of His Kingdom. By anchoring ourselves in the eternal truths of Scripture and living with an eternal perspective, we can navigate the temporal challenges of life with wisdom, grace, and purpose.

TEAMWORK

God's design for us as Kingdom Leaders is rooted in the concept of teamwork rather than individualism. While some leadership theories may center on a hierarchical structure where a few individuals control the actions of many, true teamwork transcends such paradigms. In a team-oriented approach, each member operates on an equal footing, leveraging their unique talents, gifts, and abilities to inspire, support, develop, and uplift others.

Rather than a top-down leadership style, teamwork fosters a collaborative environment where every individual contributes their strengths toward a common goal. It is about recognizing and valuing the diverse contributions of each team member, empowering everyone to lead in their own capacity and to collectively achieve greater success. This cooperative spirit mirrors the essence of Kingdom Leadership, where humility, service, and mutual respect are the guiding principles.

This aspect of Kingdom Leadership, rooted in teamwork and collaboration, holds significant importance to God and is indeed reflected in the very act of creation. In Genesis 2:18, we encounter the moment when God declares that it is not good for man to be alone, highlighting the inherent need for companionship and collaboration.

> *"Then the Lord God said, "It is not good that the man should be alone; I will make him a helper fit for him."*

From the outset, God recognized that we could not fulfill His purposes alone. Thus, He designed us to thrive in community, where we can both receive and give assistance. The narrative in Genesis illustrates this principle through God's deliberate creation of companionship for Adam, culminating in the creation of Woman. Beyond this individual instance, it speaks to the broader concept of mutual support and servanthood among all humanity. As Kingdom Leaders, our role is not to dictate or control, but to serve one another, uplifting and empowering each person to fulfill their God-given potential.

Why do we, as Kingdom Leaders, require one another? It is because the Body of Christ is composed of numerous parts, each with its designated role to fulfill. In 1 Corinthians 12:12, we encounter the analogy of the body used to illustrate the interconnectedness and interdependence of believers within the Church.

> *"For just as the body is one and has many members, and all the members of the body, though many, are one body...."*

Teamwork is indispensable for a Kingdom Leader, as no single individual can fulfill all the diverse functions required. Consider the typical Sunday service at the church many of us attend. There are door greeters, kitchen servers, cleaners, kids and youth ministry leaders, sound and music team members, preachers, and numerous other roles that contribute to the smooth operation of the Church. It is evident no one person can fulfill all these responsibilities on their own, not just on a Sunday morning, but throughout the week as well. Each part plays a crucial role, and if any one of them were to falter, the overall effectiveness of the Church would be compromised.

The success of the Church, and ultimately the promotion of the Kingdom of Heaven, hinges on each member operating in alignment with their purpose, utilizing their talents, gifts, and abilities to their fullest extent. As Kingdom Leaders, it is imperative we function within the collaborative framework of the church community. Only by working together harmoniously can we fulfill our collective mission and effectively advance the Kingdom of Heaven.

To be effective Kingdom Leaders within the Church and the Body of Christ, it is crucial for us to actively engage in attending and participating in gatherings. These meetings serve as valuable opportunities for us to receive encouragement, support, and guidance as we continue to pursue God's purpose in our lives. Hebrews 10:24-25 indeed extends this encouragement, urging believers not to neglect meeting together, but to spur one another on toward love and good deeds, especially as the day of Christ's return draws nearer.

> *"And let us consider how to stir up one another to love and good works, not neglecting to meet together, as is the habit of some, but encouraging one another…."*

1 Thessalonians 5:11 also inspires us to encourage and build up one another, just as we are called to do, reinforcing the importance of community and mutual support within the Body of Christ.

> *"Therefore encourage one another and build one another up…."*

Kingdom Leadership is inherently relational, emphasizing the significance of maintaining strong connections with those around us. These connections serve as vital conduits for mutual encouragement, support, and growth. By actively engaging with others, we not only receive the encouragement and assistance we need to persevere in our own journey, but we can also extend Kingdom Leadership to others.

As Kingdom Leaders, we recognize the intrinsic value of every individual within our community and seek to foster a culture of collaboration, empathy, and empowerment. We understand that we are stronger together than we are alone and that our collective efforts are essential for achieving shared goals and objectives.

Staying connected within the Body of Christ is essential for effectively promoting the Kingdom of Heaven here on earth. When we operate from our God-given purpose and utilize our talents, gifts, and abilities within the context of community, we maximize our effectiveness in advancing God's Kingdom.

By staying connected, we not only receive the support, encouragement, and accountability needed to fulfill our roles as Kingdom Leaders but can also collaborate with others in shared mission and vision. Through our collective efforts and unified purpose, we amplify our impact and reach far beyond what we could ever achieve alone.

In essence, our connection within the Body of Christ enables us to be effective ambassadors of God's Kingdom, actively contributing to its expansion and transformation here on earth. As we operate in unity, utilizing our unique gifts and abilities for the greater good, we bear witness to the power and presence of God at work among us.

PATIENCE

Throughout the day, a Kingdom Leader encounters numerous challenges that can trigger intense emotions, potentially affecting those around them.

Whether it is dealing with tardiness, missing deliveries, conflicts, or subpar performance, these situations can have a significant impact on a person's emotional state. As a result, a Kingdom Leader may find themselves on the brink of emotional overload.

Patience stands as a crucial trait for every Kingdom Leader to cultivate. Reflecting on earlier discussions in the book, we recognize that God has already instilled patience within us. However, it is incumbent upon us to discern the opportunities for its development.

Developing patience involves recognizing and embracing the moments and circumstances that challenge us to exercise this virtue. Whether it is navigating through delays, setbacks, or conflicts, each situation presents an opportunity for growth and refinement. Instead of succumbing to frustration or impatience, a Kingdom Leader is called to approach these challenges with a spirit of resilience, perseverance, and trust in God's timing and providence.

Proverbs 15:18 serves as a valuable reminder for Kingdom Leaders to keep their emotions in check, especially in tense situations. Committing this scripture to memory can provide a guiding light in moments of conflict or frustration, helping to diffuse tension and promote peace.

> *"A hot-tempered man stirs up strife, but he who is slow to anger quiets contention."*

As Kingdom Leaders, cultivating patience, particularly the ability to be slow to anger, is paramount. This type of patience empowers us to exercise restraint in moments of tension or conflict, creating space for calmness and rationality to prevail. By remaining composed and level-headed, even in challenging circumstances, we can effectively de-escalate situations and facilitate constructive dialogue, fostering understanding and collaboration among those involved.

Exercising patience in a situation not only enables a Kingdom Leader to maintain composure but also enhances their ability to gain deeper understanding and discern the most appropriate course of action. Rushing into decisions impulsively can often lead to hasty or ill-informed choices that fail to yield the desired outcomes.

In contrast, by taking the time to listen attentively, gather relevant information, and reflect thoughtfully on the situation, a Kingdom Leader can make more informed and deliberate decisions. This patient approach allows for thorough evaluation and consideration of various perspectives, ultimately leading to more effective and sustainable solutions.

Thus, patience serves as a valuable tool for Kingdom Leaders, empowering them to navigate challenges with wisdom, discernment, and grace. Proverbs 18:13 emphasizes this principle by highlighting the folly of responding hastily without fully understanding the matter at hand.

"If one gives an answer before he hears, it is his folly and shame."

A Kingdom Leader must possess the discernment to identify the correct decision and path forward. Acting impulsively or hastily can lead to errors or misjudgments. When advancing the Kingdom of Heaven as Kingdom Leaders, it is crucial to exercise patience, actively listen to others, and carefully consider all relevant factors—not just the apparent ones—to discern the right course of action.

Even for a Kingdom Leader, discerning the right path forward may not always be straightforward. The abundance of information to process and consider can sometimes feel overwhelming, turning the decision-making process into more of a burden than a source of joy. In such moments, a Kingdom Leader turns to God, seeking His guidance and wisdom to illuminate the way forward.

By entrusting the complexities of decision-making to God and relying on His divine guidance and answers, a Kingdom Leader finds reassurance, clarity, and direction. Paul's letter to the Philippians offers encouragement and insight into navigating challenging decisions and uncertainties.

> *"Do not be anxious about anything, but in everything by prayer and supplication with thanksgiving let your requests be made known to God."* Philippians 4:6

As Kingdom Leaders committed to prayer, it is vital to carve out dedicated moments throughout our day to connect with God. Amidst the hustle and bustle of the workplace, finding opportunities to pause and seek divine guidance can make a profound difference in our leadership approach.

Prayer does not always require lengthy sessions or elaborate rituals. Instead, it is about cultivating a posture of openness and receptivity to God's presence and guidance. This can be as simple as taking a moment to center ourselves, quiet our minds, and offer a heartfelt prayer for wisdom and discernment.

Integrating prayer into our daily routines serves as a powerful reminder of our dependence on God in every aspect of our leadership journey. Whether facing a challenging decision, navigating interpersonal dynamics, or seeking clarity on next steps, turning to prayer allows us to surrender our concerns and uncertainties into God's capable hands.

Exercising patience entails several key aspects in our role as Kingdom Leaders. Firstly, it involves taking the time to calm a situation rather than rushing to react. Secondly, it requires refraining from making impulsive decisions that could prove detrimental. Finally, it encompasses bringing our concerns before God, seeking His guidance and wisdom. By embodying these patience principles, we as Kingdom Leaders can significantly influence our followers and advance the Kingdom of Heaven.

ACCOUNTABILITY

As Kingdom Leaders, embracing accountability requires a deep commitment to taking ownership of our decisions and actions. It means recognizing that our leadership role comes with a profound responsibility to uphold integrity, transparency, and ethical conduct in all our endeavors. What is accountability? According to the Merriam-Webster online dictionary, accountability is defined as:

> *"The quality or state of being accountable. Especially: an obligation or willingness to accept responsibility or to account for one's actions."*

Words such as responsibility, answerability, liability, and culpability are often used interchangeably with accountability. They all convey the idea of being held accountable for one's actions, decisions, and their consequences. As Kingdom Leaders, it is essential to recognize the interconnectedness of these terms and understand that embracing accountability entails acknowledging the impact of our behavior and taking ownership of the outcomes, whether positive or negative.

Romans 14:12 serves as a poignant reminder that each of us will be called to account for our lives.

> *"So then each of us will give an account of himself to God."*

Similarly, Hebrews 4:13 emphasizes that nothing we do can be hidden from God's sight.

> *"And no creature is hidden from his sight, but all are naked and exposed to the eyes of him to whom we must give account."*

So, to whom do we need to be accountable? Firstly, as emphasized by the scriptures above, we are ultimately accountable to God. Romans 3:23-24 serves as a reminder that we have all sinned and fallen short of God's glory, highlighting the need for His forgiveness and grace. While there will be a time when we are held accountable before Him, it is also crucial to recognize our ongoing accountability to God during our time on earth.

When we humbly ask for His forgiveness, we are taking ownership of our choices and behaviors that have deviated from His will and standards. We recognize those moments when we prioritized our own desires over His divine guidance, leading us to fall short and stumble into sin.

However, it is crucial to understand that God's response to our shortcomings is not one of condemnation, but of loving conviction. His aim is not to shame or criticize us, but to gently guide us back onto the path of righteousness.

> *"For God did not send his Son into the world to condemn the world, but in order that the world might be saved through him." John 3:17*

As Kingdom Leaders being accountable to God, we find solace in the assurance that although conviction may sometimes lead us to confront uncomfortable truths about areas needing improvement in our lives, we are not condemned.

Rather, we are recipients of His boundless forgiveness and grace. Embracing this reality, we recognize the necessity of holding ourselves accountable to God's standards if we are to fulfill our roles successfully as Kingdom Leaders.

As Kingdom Leaders, it is vital that we embrace mutual accountability within our community. Just as teamwork is essential for the effective functioning of the Body of Christ, it also fosters accountability among us on earth, strengthening our collective resolve. By surrounding ourselves with fellow believers, we create an environment conducive to growth, where we can learn from one another, share experiences, and refine our leadership skills.

In this supportive community, we hold each other to high standards, encouraging one another to uphold the principles of Kingdom Leadership and strive for excellence. Through constructive feedback, mutual support, and shared learning, we empower one another to fulfill our calling with greater effectiveness and impact. Together, we provide the encouragement, accountability, and camaraderie needed to navigate the challenges of leadership and grow in our ability to serve others selflessly.

By embracing accountability to our fellow Kingdom Leaders, we create a culture of accountability that promotes growth, resilience, and unity within the Body of Christ. As we journey together in our pursuit of Kingdom Leadership, we strengthen each other, inspire one another, and ultimately, advance the Kingdom of God here on earth.

Proverbs 27:17 reminds us of the importance of having others speaking into our lives.

"Iron sharpens iron, and one man sharpens another."

Engaging with fellow followers of Christ allows us to learn from seasoned Kingdom Leaders, sharpening our own leadership skills. By following their example, we grow stronger and are equipped to serve others effectively. As we receive guidance and encouragement, we in turn pass on what we have learned, perpetuating a cycle of growth within the community. Ultimately, this mutual support fosters a culture of empowerment, enabling us to fulfill our calling as Kingdom Leaders and advance God's Kingdom.

Having a supportive community of fellow believers is crucial for discerning the right course of action as a Kingdom Leader, especially in challenging situations requiring patience and wisdom. Turning to trusted individuals for guidance and counsel allows us to gain perspective and clarity, helping us navigate difficult circumstances with greater insight.

Proverbs 15:22 underscores the value of seeking counsel from others, emphasizing that wise guidance from those we trust can lead to better decisions and outcomes. By engaging in open and honest discussions with fellow Kingdom Leaders, we can explore different perspectives, weigh options, and discern the most appropriate next steps.

> *"Without counsel plans fail, but with many advisers they succeed." Proverbs 15:22*

Accountability is a vital aspect of Kingdom Leadership, anchoring us within God's grace as we strive to advance His Kingdom on earth. To thrive in this lifestyle, it is essential to surround ourselves with the right individuals—fellow Kingdom Leaders who can sharpen and fortify us in our mission.

These trusted peers serve as invaluable allies, offering guidance, support, and encouragement along our leadership journey. They hold us accountable to our commitments, challenge us to grow in character and competence, and provide constructive feedback to facilitate our development as Kingdom Leaders.

By cultivating relationships with such accountability partners, we foster a culture of mutual support and accountability within our community of believers. Together, we uphold one another in our devotion to serving God, faithfully, and promoting His Kingdom with integrity and humility.

Accountability is vital for Kingdom Leaders. It ensures alignment with God's will and promotes the advancement of His Kingdom. Trusted companions help refine plans and decisions, offering insights and keeping us grounded in our faith.

Through open dialogue and accountability, we gain clarity and stay committed to our values. This synergy between divine guidance and human support empowers us to lead with wisdom and integrity, navigating challenges with confidence as we seek to expand the Kingdom of Heaven.

INTEGRITY

One of the most glaring shortcomings in leadership, particularly evident in the political sphere, is the absence of integrity. During election campaigns, politicians frequently make grandiose promises without considering the feasibility of fulfilling them. This practice erodes trust among constituents and exposes a fundamental lack of accountability. Despite the inherent complexities of governance, some leaders resort to making excuses to justify their inability to deliver on their pledges. However, this merely underscores their deficiency in integrity and exacerbates public disillusionment.

The issue of integrity extends beyond politics and permeates various sectors, including business. In the corporate world, leaders often make lofty commitments regarding future operations, employee rewards, or financial transparency. However, some falter in upholding these promises, either due to unforeseen challenges or, regrettably, personal greed. This breach of trust not only undermines the morale of employees but also jeopardizes the long-term sustainability of the organization. Instances of embezzlement or fraudulent financial practices further underscore the erosion of integrity among business leaders, highlighting the urgent need for ethical leadership and accountability.

God finds joy when we demonstrate integrity in our interactions and conduct with others. He takes pleasure in our commitment to righteousness, even in the privacy of our hearts and minds.

> *"I know, my God, that you test the heart and have pleasure in uprightness." 1 Chronicles 29:17*

Operating with integrity means consistently adhering to moral and ethical principles, even when faced with difficult circumstances or temptations. As Kingdom Leaders, this entails staying true to our values and commitments in all aspects of life, whether at home, in the workplace, within our community, or at church.

Integrity involves being honest and transparent in our interactions, keeping our promises, and upholding ethical standards even when no one is watching. It is about doing what is right, even if it comes at a personal cost or inconvenience. This commitment to integrity is not just about external actions but also reflects the inner character and values of a Kingdom Leader.

In a world where self-interest often dominates, maintaining integrity can be challenging. There may be temptations to compromise our principles for personal gain or to avoid consequences. However, as Kingdom Leaders, we are called to emulate the integrity exemplified by Jesus Christ, who remained steadfast in his values and principles even in the face of adversity.

Drawing closer to God through prayer, meditation on scripture, and seeking His guidance enables Kingdom Leaders to uphold integrity consistently. It is through this spiritual connection that we find strength, wisdom, and discernment to navigate the complexities of leadership with integrity.

Psalm 25:20-21 urges us to seek refuge in God's presence.

> *"Oh, guard my soul, and deliver me! Let me not be put to shame, for I take refuge in you. May integrity and uprightness preserve me, for I wait for you."*

Drawing close to God enables Him to protect our soul, delivering us from the snares of the world and providing refuge so that we do not face shame. Integrity acts as a shield, preventing accusations against our actions and decisions. As Kingdom Leaders, maintaining integrity preserves and upholds us, setting a path for eternity, regardless of how others may treat or perceive us.

> *"But you have upheld me because of my integrity and set me in your presence forever." Psalm 41:12*

Integrity serves as a protective shield for Kingdom Leaders, safeguarding them against accusations, misrepresentations, and wrongful claims. It acts as a cloak, shielding them from the fiery arrows launched by the enemy. As Kingdom Leaders draw near to God and seek His guidance, they find refuge in Him, finding solace and strength in His presence.

Daniel's commitment to integrity led him to face opposition and jealousy from those around him, particularly in his role in the Babylonian government. Despite his exemplary character, some officials conspired against him, seeking to exploit his devotion to God for their own gain. However, Daniel's integrity remained unshaken. Similarly, Kingdom Leaders today may encounter opposition and challenges to their integrity, especially when their values conflict with those around them. Yet, like Daniel, they can remain steadfast, trusting in God's protection and ultimately bringing honor to His name.

Maintaining integrity as Kingdom Leaders is paramount, regardless of the consequences we may face. While being fired from our jobs due to our commitment to integrity can indeed bring challenges and difficulties, we must remember that our work is ultimately ordained by God. As Kingdom Leaders, our actions and decisions are guided by a higher purpose, and our dedication to integrity reflects our devotion to serving God and promoting His Kingdom. Even in the face of adversity, we can trust that God will provide for us and guide us through any challenges that may arise.

Our purpose as Kingdom Leaders, ordained by God, remains steadfast regardless of any earthly challenges we may face. Maintaining integrity enables us to continue fulfilling our role in promoting the Kingdom of Heaven and guiding others, even in the face of adversity. Our commitment to integrity ensures that we stay true to our calling and continue to serve faithfully, knowing that our ultimate accountability is to God, who sustains and empowers us in our journey as Kingdom Leaders.

SELF-DEVELOPMENT

To fully embrace Kingdom Leadership, it is imperative to prioritize continuous growth and self-development. Stagnation in knowledge, wisdom, and skill development hinders our ability to effectively serve others and fulfill our purpose. When we cease to grow, we inadvertently restrict the impact God can make through us, limiting our capacity to contribute meaningfully to His work.

Continuously seeking self-improvement is essential for enhancing our effectiveness as Kingdom Leaders. Hebrews 5:12-14 illustrates this journey of spiritual growth, emphasizing the importance of progressing from foundational truths to deeper understanding. Just as we advance in our understanding of Scripture, we must also evolve in our leadership skills and character development to better serve those around us.

> *"For though by this time you ought to be teachers, you need someone to teach you again the basic principles of the oracles of God. You need milk, not solid food, for everyone who lives on milk is unskilled in the word of righteousness, since he is a child. But solid food is for the mature, for those who have their powers of discernment trained by constant practice to distinguish good from evil." Hebrews 5:12-14*

As Kingdom Leaders, our journey of growth and self-improvement is a lifelong endeavor. It requires us to continuously seek out opportunities to deepen our understanding of spiritual truths and enhance our leadership skills. Just like infant's transition from milk to solid food as they mature, we too must progress from basic teachings to more profound insights into God's Word and His purposes.

Hebrews 5:12-14 highlights this progression, emphasizing the importance of moving beyond elementary teachings to grasp deeper spiritual truths. As we mature in our faith, we develop the discernment to distinguish between good and evil, enabling us to make wise decisions and lead others effectively.

However, this growth does not happen in isolation. Teamwork plays a crucial role in our self-development as Kingdom Leaders. By surrounding ourselves with fellow believers who are also committed to growth, we create an environment where we can challenge and encourage one another. Through mutual support and accountability, we sharpen our skills and deepen our understanding of God's Word.

As we nurture and expand our talents, gifts, and abilities, it is crucial to stay connected to Christ. Just as a branch relies on the vine for sustenance and productivity, we must maintain our connection to Him to flourish and yield abundant fruit. In John 15:5, Jesus emphasizes the importance of abiding in Him, stating that apart from Him, we can do nothing.

> "I am the vine; you are the branches. Whoever abides in me and I in him, he it is that bears much fruit, for apart from me you can do nothing."

Remaining close to Christ involves daily practices such as prayer, meditation on Scripture, and cultivating a heart of worship. These disciplines not only deepen our relationship with God but also provide us with the spiritual nourishment and guidance needed to navigate the complexities of Kingdom Leadership. Additionally, seeking fellowship with other believers and participating in Christian communities can offer support, encouragement, and accountability on our journey of growth and service. By prioritizing our connection with Christ, we position ourselves to bear fruit that glorifies Him and advances His Kingdom in the world.

Finding time for self-development can indeed be challenging amidst life's distractions. Various demands and tasks often vie for our attention, making it easy to neglect personal growth. However, prioritizing this aspect of our journey as Kingdom Leaders is crucial. Without a commitment to ongoing growth, we risk stagnation in our leadership roles. Therefore, it is vital to carve out dedicated time for self-improvement, ensuring continuous progress and effectiveness in our service. Paul's encouragement to Timothy remains relevant for us today, urging us to pursue personal and spiritual growth with diligence.

> *"Practice these things, immerse yourself in them, so that all may see your progress." 1 Timothy 4:15*

By consistently honing our skills and talents, we demonstrate a dedication to excellence that encourages others to follow suit. When they witness our progress and witness the positive impact of our efforts, they are inspired to embark on their own journeys of self-improvement. Our commitment to growth sets a powerful example, fostering a culture of continuous learning and development within our communities and organizations. As Kingdom Leaders, this dedication to personal growth not only benefits us individually but also contributes to the collective advancement of those we serve.

When you consistently demonstrate Kingdom Leadership and actively engage in self-improvement, you radiate a compelling presence that naturally draws others to you. People are inspired by your dedication to growth and service, and they instinctively gravitate toward your example. Your diligent efforts to refine your talents, nurture your gifts, and enhance your abilities serve as a beacon of encouragement, motivating others to embark on their own journey of personal and spiritual development.

As you continue to lead by example, your influence expands, touching the lives of those around you and igniting a collective passion for advancing the Kingdom of Heaven. Through your unwavering commitment to growth and service, you create a ripple effect of positive change, inspiring others to discover their potential and contribute to a greater purpose.

In essence, by embodying Kingdom Leadership and embracing continuous self-improvement, you not only empower yourself to reach new heights but also empower others to do the same. Together, you form a community of dedicated individuals united in their pursuit of excellence and their desire to make a meaningful impact in the world for the Kingdom of Heaven.

DISCIPLINE

When people hear the word "discipline," it often evokes thoughts of punishment or correction. Many of us associate discipline with past experiences of being reprimanded for mistakes or misbehavior during childhood. Due to this negative connotation, we tend to view discipline as something to be avoided or rejected in our lives.

According to the Merriam-Webster online dictionary, discipline encompasses various definitions regarding its expression.

1. a: control gained by enforcing obedience or order
   b: orderly or prescribed conduct or pattern of behavior
   c: self-control
2. punishment

3. training that corrects, molds, or perfects the mental faculties or moral character
4. a field of study
5. a rule of system of rules governing conduct activity

Typically, as mentioned earlier, our understanding of discipline has primarily centered on its second defined aspect, punishment. Due to our negative experiences with discipline, we have come to believe it as something negative. Consequently, our convictions, attitudes, perceptions, and behaviors have aligned accordingly. In Hebrews 12:11, the writer acknowledges the challenge inherent in embracing discipline.

> *"For the moment all discipline seems painful rather than pleasant, but later it yields the peaceful fruit of righteousness to those who have been trained by it."*

Experiencing discipline, while often challenging, offers a valuable opportunity for growth and understanding. In Hebrews 12:11, the author not only acknowledges the difficulty inherent in discipline but also invites deeper reflection by highlighting the specific Greek term used: "Paideia." This word speaks to a holistic approach to correction and guidance, akin to a parent's loving instruction of their child.

When exploring the concept of "Paideia," we uncover layers of meaning that extend beyond mere correction. It embodies a sense of care and concern, reflecting the parental desire to nurture and educate their offspring. Just as a devoted parent seeks to steer their child toward maturity and wisdom through patient instruction, so too does the Father's discipline aim to mold us into better versions of ourselves.

In understanding "Paideia," we recognize that discipline is not merely about punishment or retribution but rather about transformation and growth. It is about cultivating virtues, instilling wisdom, and fostering resilience. Like a skilled artisan shaping a piece of raw material into a work of art, discipline molds and refines us, shaping our character and guiding our journey toward spiritual maturity in Christ.

Moreover, the parental aspect inherent in "Paideia" reminds us of the relationship between the discipliner and the disciplined. It implies a bond of love and trust, wherein correction is offered not out of cruelty or indifference but out of a genuine desire for the well-being and flourishing of the individual.

Therefore, while the process of discipline may indeed be unpleasant at times, it is ultimately grounded in love and intended for our benefit. Embracing the lessons embedded within "Paideia," we can approach discipline with humility and gratitude, knowing that through it, we are being shaped into the image of our loving Father.

When interpreted in this manner, the meaning of discipline shifts from the punitive connotation we may have initially linked with the scripture, toward the definition outlined in point three of the Merriam-Webster Dictionary: one of training, molding, or refining the state of mind or moral character.

By incorporating discipline into our lives as Kingdom Leaders, we open ourselves to God's guidance and instruction, akin to a parent nurturing, correcting, and guiding their child. This allows us to learn how to fulfill the calling of effective leadership as ordained by God.

How can we discern if God is exercising discipline as a loving parent, rather than employing punishment as a tyrannical overlord? In Hebrews 12:7, earlier in the same chapter, we encounter the following passage:

> *"It is for discipline that you have to endure. God is treating you as sons. For what son is there whom his father does not discipline?"*

In Hebrews 12:7, the continuity of the Greek term "Paideia" underscores its significance in understanding divine discipline. This word encapsulates the multifaceted approach of training, guiding, and instructing akin to a parent's care for their child's development. When applied to our relationship with God, it illuminates His role as a compassionate and nurturing Father, deeply invested in our growth and well-being.

Imagine a devoted parent patiently teaching their child life's lessons, not through harsh punishment but through gentle guidance and firm instruction. Similarly, God's discipline reflects His desire to mold us into individuals of integrity, wisdom, and compassion. His guidance is not driven by a desire to control or dominate but rather by a deep love that seeks our flourishing.

As our heavenly Father, God knows us intimately, understanding our strengths, weaknesses, and potential. Therefore, His discipline is always tailored to our needs, aimed at cultivating the qualities necessary for us to fulfill our purpose as Kingdom Leaders. Through His guidance, we learn not only how to navigate the complexities of life but also how to lead with humility, empathy, and grace.

For Kingdom Leaders, cultivating the same type of discipline within their lives is crucial for bearing the fruit of righteousness. This is significant because we are recognized by the fruits we bear. Our actions serve as a reflection of our character and values to those around us. If our actions lack discipline and are not aligned with the guidance and instruction of our heavenly Father, we risk straying from His intended purpose for us.

Kingdom Leaders are called to embody the values of the Kingdom of Heaven through their words, deeds, and character. This requires a disciplined approach to life, characterized by obedience to God's will, integrity, humility, and love. Without such discipline, our actions may become self-serving, inconsistent, or even harmful, leading others to question the authenticity of our faith and the relevance of the Kingdom we represent.

By cultivating discipline in our lives, we align ourselves with God's purpose and demonstrate our commitment to His Kingdom values. This not only strengthens our own spiritual journey but also enables us to effectively serve as ambassadors of Christ's love and grace in the world. Our disciplined actions become a testimony to the transformative power of God's grace, drawing others closer to Him and reflecting His glory to the world.

How can we initiate the process of incorporating discipline into our lives? It starts with acknowledging our need for discipline and embracing the necessity of implementing the "Paideia" discipline daily. Proverbs 12:1 straightforwardly addresses the consequences for those who fail to acknowledge the importance of discipline in their lives.

> *"Whoever loves discipline loves knowledge, but he who hates reproof is stupid."*

Embracing "Paideia" discipline is not merely a choice but a fundamental necessity in our journey toward fulfilling our role as Kingdom Leaders according to God's divine plan. From the very inception of creation, God's intention has been for humanity to steward His creation and manifest His Kingdom on earth. Throughout the pages of Scripture, from Genesis to Revelation, this overarching narrative reveals God's desire for His people to live as servants in Kingdom Leadership, reflecting His love, justice, and compassion to the world.

In this grand narrative, discipline plays a central role. It is through the process of "Paideia" discipline that we are shaped and molded into the image-bearers of God, equipped to carry out His redemptive work in the world. Just as a skilled artisan meticulously refines a piece of clay into a masterpiece, God's discipline refines our character, purifies our motives, and strengthens our resolve to walk in His ways.

Learning to love "Paideia" discipline involves a shift in perspective—a recognition that discipline is not a burden to be avoided but a gift to be embraced. It is through discipline that we are empowered to overcome our weaknesses, grow in maturity, and align our lives with God's purposes. As Kingdom Leaders, our ability to lead with humility, integrity, and grace is contingent upon our willingness to submit to God's discipline and allow it to shape us into vessels of His Kingdom.

CHAPTER REFLECTION

Scriptures to Read

1 Corinthians 12	Matthew 25:14-30	Psalm 139:13
Ephesians 4:32	1 John 3:18	Matthew 5:9
Genesis 1:27	Isaiah 64:8	Psalm 139:14
Exodus 35:35	Exodus 31:3-5	Proverbs 22:29
1 Peter 4:10	Psalm 39:4	Ephesians 5:15-17
2 Corinthians 4:18	Colossians 4:5	Genesis 2:18
Hebrews 10:24-25	1 Thessalonians 5:11	Proverbs 15:18
Proverbs 18:13	Philippians 4:6	Romans 14:12
Hebrews 4:13	Romans 3:23-24	John 3:17
Proverbs 27:17	Proverbs 15:22	1 Chronicles 29:17
Psalm 25:20-21	Psalm 41:12	Hebrews 5:12-14
John 15:5	1 Timothy 4:15	Hebrews 12:11
Hebrews 12:7	Proverbs 12:1	

Key Concepts

- As Kingdom Leaders, it is crucial to use our talents, gifts, and abilities for His Kingdom, as illustrated in Jesus' parables.
- Failure to utilize these may prevent us from fulfilling our purpose according to His will.
- Serving people outside the Church through your talents, gifts, and abilities, can have as much an impact as serving those within.
- Be innovative in your approach to serving as a Kingdom Leader.
- Manage your time effectively to maximize opportunities.
- Work collaboratively within the Body of Christ to thrive as a Kingdom Leader.

- Practice patience with yourself, your family, your Church, and the broader community.
- Seek accountability from trusted individuals as you grow in your role as a Kingdom Leader.
- Maintain integrity in all aspects of your leadership—it is a lifestyle, not just a role.
- Continuously pursue personal growth to empower yourself and those around you.
- Embrace daily discipline as a means of growth and development in your journey as a Kingdom Leader.

CHAPTER SEVEN

KINGDOM LEADERSHIP SUMMARY

As you have journeyed through this book, I trust you have devoted moments to reflecting on the notion of Kingdom Leadership, perhaps contemplating its implications for your own life. My aspiration is that it has served to uplift, motivate, and potentially reshape your understanding of your role as a Kingdom Leader within God's Kingdom.

Each of you holds a position of leadership within the tapestry of God's divine plan, crafted with purpose and precision by the hands of the Creator. You are not here by chance, but by design, with a distinct combination of talents, gifts, and abilities intricately woven into the fabric of your being. God, in His infinite wisdom, has bestowed upon you these unique qualities to fulfill a specific role in His grand narrative.

As you navigate through life, it is essential to recognize the inherent value that you possess as a beloved child of God. Your self-worth is not contingent upon external validation or worldly achievements but is rooted deeply in your identity as a cherished creation of the Almighty. Embrace the truth of your worthiness and allow it to fuel your confidence as you step into your leadership role.

Confidence in oneself is not arrogance or self-importance but a recognition of the divine potential within. It is a quiet assurance that you are equipped and empowered by God to fulfill the purpose for which you were created. With this confidence, you can navigate life's challenges with courage and resilience, knowing you are supported by the Creator of the universe.

Furthermore, cultivate a healthy self-esteem grounded in a balanced understanding of your strengths and weaknesses. Acknowledge your talents and abilities as gifts from God, to be stewarded wisely for the betterment of others and the advancement of His Kingdom. At the same time, be humble enough to recognize areas where growth and improvement are needed, relying on God's grace and guidance to refine and develop your character.

As you embrace the principles of Kingdom Leadership, remember that it is not merely a set of techniques to be learned but a way of life to be lived. It involves a radical shift in perspective, from self-centeredness to other centeredness, from seeking recognition to serving with humility and love. Allow the values of Kingdom Leadership to permeate every aspect of your existence, shaping your thoughts, words, and actions in alignment with the example set forth by Jesus Christ.

When practicing Kingdom Leadership, it is crucial to understand that it does not entail controlling or manipulating others to fulfill our own desires. We are not called by God to exercise dominion over people; rather, our calling is to serve as humble leaders in His Kingdom. By serving one another selflessly, we bear fruits of love, kindness, and compassion, which serve as a beacon to those outside the Church, drawing them closer to God.

KINGDOM LEADERSHIP SUMMARY

Cultivating a mindset of Kingdom Leadership requires intentional effort and daily renewal of our thoughts. Take time each day to reflect on your identity as a leader, grounded in Christ's example of servanthood. Allow this belief to permeate your consciousness, shaping your convictions and attitudes toward Kingdom Leadership.

Shift your convictions so that you confidently embody Kingdom Leadership in every aspect of your life. Regardless of the circumstances—whether you are having a good day or a bad one—let your perception of Kingdom Leadership remain positive and unwavering. Recognize it as a profound and transformative force within your life, one that brings about goodness and blessing to those around you.

As you internalize this mindset, let it influence your behavior and interactions with others. Approach every situation with confidence, knowing that as a Kingdom Leader you are fulfilling the calling placed upon you by God. Your actions and demeanor will reflect this confidence, inspiring others and drawing them closer to the heart of Kingdom Leadership.

In essence, by renewing your mind daily and embracing your identity as a Kingdom Leader in Christ, you will experience a profound transformation in your attitudes, beliefs, and behaviors toward leadership. With confidence and conviction, you will radiate the essence of Kingdom Leadership, becoming a beacon of light and hope in a world in need of God's love and grace.

Dedicate time in prayer and meditation, allowing God to reveal the talents, gifts, and abilities He has uniquely bestowed on you. Tap into your creative potential, exploring and nurturing the creative streak hidden within you. Ensure effective time management to maximize productivity and fulfill your responsibilities.

Work collaboratively within a team, both within the Church and in various aspects of your life, offering Kingdom Leadership in areas where you excel while humbly following the lead of others in areas where you perceive weaknesses. Exercise patience with yourself as you grow and extend patience to those around you.

Embrace accountability as a means of personal and spiritual growth, ensuring transparency and integrity in all your dealings. Remain steadfast in your commitment to uphold moral and ethical standards, resisting the temptations of the world that seek to undermine your integrity.

Continuously seek opportunities for personal and leadership development, focusing on enhancing the specific talents, gifts, and abilities entrusted to you by God. Let your leadership journey be marked by a spirit of humility, growth, and unwavering dedication to serving others with excellence and compassion.

Make sure to integrate "Paideia" into your daily routine. Each day offers you the chance to embrace this discipline, allowing God to train, guide, and instruct you in utilizing the talents, gifts, and abilities He has bestowed upon you. Seek out a Kingdom Leader who shares similarities with you, granted by God, and learn from their example. This way, you can grow and develop, as you become a Kingdom Leader to others, fulfilling your calling and expanding the Kingdom of God on earth.

As you navigate your path in leadership, it is vital to maintain a perspective rooted in the understanding that your service occurs within the Kingdom of Heaven. Here, God stands as the sovereign King, holding ultimate authority over all things. Regardless of your role or position, it is essential to recognize that it is not about personal status or ambition; rather, it is about aligning your actions and decisions with God's purpose for your life.

In every aspect of your leadership journey, remind yourself that you are a steward of the authority entrusted to you by God. God's desire to govern the earth through His Kingdom is a profound privilege for those called to be part of it. Stewarding His authority on earth as a Kingdom Leader is a responsibility of immense value while He reigns over His Kingdom. Answering God's call to expand His Kingdom by fulfilling Jesus' command to spread the Gospel to all nations and make disciples is made possible through the gracious delegation of authority to those who willingly acknowledge and submit to His lordship.

This call does not demand perfection from you as a Kingdom Leader but acknowledging that to succeed you may require a transformation of mindset leading to a change in behavior. Striving to daily renew the mind, understanding that leadership, power, and influence within the Kingdom are not self-generated but graciously bestowed upon you by His grace. Live to Kingdom principles of integrity, transparency, ethical conduct, humility, and compassion in all aspects of life. This enables you as a Kingdom Leader to foster humility, guard against pride, and keep your heart aligned with His purpose.

Embrace the truth that your service is ultimately directed toward advancing God's Kingdom agenda on earth. Every decision, every action should reflect His values of love, justice, and compassion. Seek His guidance and wisdom in all things, acknowledging His sovereignty and submitting to His divine will.

As we humbly submit ourselves to Him on earth, faithfully serving as Kingdom Leaders and persevering in the race until the end, my prayer is that both you and I will hear the words, *"... Well done, good and faithful servant ...."* Matthew 25:23

ACKNOWLEDGEMENTS

First and foremost, to my wife, who saw in me more than I even realized was there. Your unwavering love, support, and dedication have been a constant source of strength for me. Thank you for your care and for walking this journey of faith alongside me, sharing a deep desire to know God more intimately together.

My parents, whose faithfulness in taking me to church laid a strong foundation for my own journey. Thank you for encouraging me not only to attend but also to seek ways to serve and grow. Your guidance and support have instilled in me a desire to give back and live out my faith.

Uncle Laurie and Auntie Jan Milborn, my Sunday school teachers: thank you for your faithfulness and dedication in teaching so many, especially me. Your willingness to share and build a foundation of faith in my life has been invaluable.

Laurie and Deva Chapman, thank you for the instrumental mentoring you provided during my late teens and twenties. I am deeply grateful for the time and effort you invested in helping me stay focused on becoming the man God has called me to be.

Finally, to God for *"He has made everything beautiful in its time...."* *Ecclesiastes 3:11*. I do not always understand why things happen the way they do or why I face certain challenges. In those moments of uncertainty, it can be difficult to see the bigger picture. However, whenever I reflect on what You have accomplished in my life, I realize – it is always beautiful.

ENDNOTES

Annas, Juila. 2003. "Plato: A very Short Introduction". *Oxford University Press*. Oxford, New York. https://ap01.alma.exlibrisgroup.com/view/delivery/61CUR_INST/12193963770001951

Athanassoulis, Nafsika. "Virtue Ethics". *The Internet Encyclopedia of Philosophy*, ISSN 2161-0002, https://www.iep.utm.edu/, 13 September 2020.

Bacha, Eliane, Sandra Walker. 2013. "The Relationship Between Transformation Leadership and Followers' Perceptions of Fairness". *Journal of Business Ethics* 116 (3): 667-680. http://www.jstor.com/stable/42001949

Bass, Bernard M. and Bruce J. Avolio. 1993. "Transformational Leadership and Organizational Culture." *Public Administration Quarterly* 17 (1): 112. https://link.library.curtin.edu.au/gw?url=https://www-proquest-com.dbgw.lis.curtin.edu.au/docview/226966626?accountid=10382

Bert, Alan Spector. 2015. "Carlyle, Freud, and the Great Man Theory more fully considered". *Leadership*. 12 (2), 250-260. https://doi.org/10.1177/1742715015571392

Bertrand, Russell. 1967. "The Problems of Philosophy". *Oxford University Press*. Great Britain. https://ap01.alma.exlibrisgroup.com/view/delivery/61CUR_INST/12182058810001951

Cairns, T.D., Hollenback, J., Preziosi, R.C. and Snow, W.A. 1998. "Technical note: a study of Hersey and Blanchard's situational leadership theory". *Leadership & Organization Development Journal.* 19 (2): 113-116. https://doi.org/10.1108/01437739810208692

Calhoun, Cheshire. 1995. "Standing for Something". *The Journal of Philosophy* 92 (5): 235-260. https://doi-org.dbgw.lis.curtin.edu.au/10.2307/2940917

Copp, David. 2007. "The Oxford Handbook of Ethical Theory". *Oxford University Press.* Oxford, New York. https://www-oxfordhandbooks-com.dbgw.lis.curtin.edu.au/view/10.1093/oxfordhb/9780195325911.001.0001/oxfordhb-9780195325911-e-1

Dr. Joseph Murphy, *The Power of your Subconscious Mind* (London: Simon & Schuster, 2018)

Dr. Myles Munroe, *The Spirit of Leadership: Cultivating the attitudes that Influence Human Action* (New Kensington, Pennsylvania: Whitaker House, 2005)

Dr. Myles Munroe, *Understanding the Purpose and Power of Men: God's Design for Male Identity* (New Kensington, Pennsylvania: Whitaker House, 2001, 2017)

Ebener, Dan R., David J. O'Connell. 2010. "How Might Servant Leadership Work?". *Nonprofit Management and Leadership* 20(3): 315-336. http://web.b.ebscohost.com.dbgw.lis.curtin.edu.au/ehost/detail/detail?vid=2&sid=77c9141c-3b0e-4988-a120-779a9e1c993e%40pdc-v-sessmgr06&bdata=JnNpdGU9ZWhvc3QtbGl2ZQ%3d%3d#AN=48490646&db=bth

Gentile, Mary C. 2010. "Giving Voice to Values". *Yale University Press, New Haven.* https://ebookcentral.proquest.com/lib/curtin/reader.action?docID=3420959

Gronum, Nico J. 2015. "A Return to Virtue Ethics: Virtue Ethics, Cognitive Science And Character Education". *Verbum et Ecclesia* 36 (1): 1-6. https://search-proquest-com.dbgw.lis.curtin.edu.au/docview/1737513896?rfr_id=info%3Axri%2Fsid%3Aprimo

Hemsworth, David, Jonathan Muterera, Anahita Laramie. 2013. "Examining Bass's Transformational Leadership in Public Sector Executives: A Psychometric Properties Review". *Journal of Applied Business Research* 29 (3): 853. https://search-proquest-com.dbgw.lis.curtin.edu.au/docview/1370363950?rfr_id=info%3Axri%2Fsid%3Aprimo

Janse, Ben. 2019. "Great Man Theory of Leadership". *Toolshero.* https://www.toolshero.com/leadership/great-man-theory/

John C. Maxwell, *The 21 Irrefutable Laws of Leadership: follow them and people will follow you* (Nashville, Tennessee: Nelson Books, 1998, 2007)

John C. Maxwell, *What Successful People Know about Leadership* (New York, New York: Centre Street, 2016)

John C. Maxwell, *How Successful People Think* (New York, New York: Centre Street, 2009)

Jones, Rebecca J., Stephen A. Woods, Yves R. F. Guillaume. 2016. "The Effectiveness of Workplace Coaching: A Meta-Analysis Of Learning And Performance Outcomes From Coaching". *Journal of Occupational & Organizational Psychology* 89 (2): 249-277. http://web.b.ebscohost.com.dbgw.lis.curtin.edu.au/ehost/detail/detail?vid=0&sid=b44f65ed-b84f-48a3-8c75-4ea8e5db7779%40pdc-v-sessmgr03&bdata=JnNpdGU9ZWhvc3QtbGl2ZQ%3d%3d#db=bth&AN=115055631

Jordan B. Peterson, *12 Rules for Life: an antidote to chaos* (Canada: Random House Canada, 2018)

Jowett, Benjamin. 2012. The Republic by Plato. Luton, Bedfordshire: Andrews UK Ltd. Accessed October 12, 2020. ProQuest eBook

Central. https://ebookcentral.proquest.com/lib/curtin/detail.action?docID=4460786#

Kant, Immanuel. 2005. "The Moral Law: Groundwork of The Metaphysics Of Morals". *Routledge.* New York. http://ebookcentral.proquest.com/lib/curtin/reader.action?docID=653009

Khan, Zubair Ahmad, Sameer Jan Bhat, and Irem Hussanie. 2017. "Understanding leadership theories - A review for researchers." *Asian Journal of Research in Social Sciences and Humanities.* 7 (5): 249-264. http://dx.doi.org/10.5958/2249-7315.2017.00313.6

Kellerman, Barbara. 2005. "How Bad Leadership Happens". Leader to Leader 2005 (35): 41-46. 10.1002/ltl.113

Korac-Kakabadse, N., Korac-Kakabadse, A., & Kouzmin, A. 200). "Leadership Renewal: Towards the Philosophy of Wisdom". *International Review of Administrative Sciences.* 67 (2): 207-227. https://doi.org/10.1177/0020852301672002

Laschinger, Heather K Spence, Carol A. Wong, Greta A. Cummings, Ashley L. Grau. "Resonant Leadership And Workplace Empowerment: The Value Of Positive Organizational Cultures In Reducing Workplace Incivility". *Nursing Economics* 32 (1): 5-15. https://search-proquest-com.dbgw.lis.curtin.edu.au/docview/1508688469/fulltextPDF/63D6BAA60BF24C74PQ/1?accountid=10382

Machiavelli, Niccolò. 2014. The Prince. Open Road Media. Accessed October 14, 2020. ProQuest Ebook Central. https://ebookcentral.proquest.com/lib/curtin/detail.action?pq-origsite=primo&docID=1807411#

McKim, Richard. 1985. "Socratic Self-Knowledge and "Knowledge of Knowledge" in Plato's Charmides". *Transactions of the American Philological Association.* 115: 59-77. https://www.jstor.org/stable/284190

Merriam-Webster Online Dictionary. 2024. https://www.merriam-webster.com/

Miller, Kiara. 2022 "A Comprehensive Guide on The Great Man Theory of Leadership". *Crowjack.* https://crowjack.com/blog/strategy/leadership-theories/great-man-theory

Möbus, Freya. 2023. "Socratic Leadership". *International Journal of Applied Philosophy.* 36 (2): 263-281. 10.5840/ijap2023717190

O'Toole, James. 1995. "Why Amoral Leadership Doesn't Work". *Jossey Bass.* San Francisco, California. https://ap01.alma.exlibrisgroup.com/view/delivery/61CUR_INST/12182005080001951

Pawar, Avinash, Khortum Sudan, Satini Satini, and Denok Sunarsi. "Organizational servant leadership." *International Journal of Educational Administration, Management, and Leadership* (2020): 63-76. https://doi.org/10.51629/ijeamal.v1i2.8

Quinn, Robert E., Sue R. Faerman, Michael P. Thompson, Michael R. McGrath, David S. Bright. 2015. *Becoming a Master Manager: A Competing Values Approach.* USA. Wiley & Sons.

Rachels, James, Stuart Rachels. 2014. "The Elements of Moral Philosophy". *McGraw-Hill.* New York. https://ebookcentral.proquest.com/lib/curtin/reader.action?docID=5471292

Robertson, Michael, Kirsty Morris, Garry Walter. 2007. "Overview Of Psychiatric Ethics V: Utilitarianism And The Ethics Of Duty". *Australasian Psychiatry* 15 (5): 1-9. https://doi-org.dbgw.lis.curtin.edu.au/10.1080/10398560701439640

Schiemann, Sandra J., Christina Muhlberger, F. David Schoorman, Eva Jones. 2019. "Trust me, I am a caring coach: The benefits of establishing trustworthiness during coaching by communicating benevolence". *Journal of Trust Research* 9 (2): 164-184.

https://doi-org.dbgw.lis.curtin.edu.au/10.1080/21515581.2019.1650751

She, Zhuolin, Bingqing Li, Quan Li, Manuel London, Baiyin Yang. 2019. "The Double-Edged Sword Of Coaching: Relationships Between

Managers' Coaching And Their Feelings Of Personal Accomplishment And Role Overload". *Human Resource Development Quarterly* 30 (2): 245-266. http://web.b.ebscohost.com.dbgw.lis.curtin.edu.au/ehost/detail/detail?vid=0&sid=f701ec5b-2518-4cc5-8a3a-bbec193e5d2a%40pdc-v-sessmgr02&bdata=JnNpdGU9ZWhvc3QtbGl2ZQ%3d%3d#db=bth&AN=136837868

Sims, Cynthia, Angela Carter, Arelis Moore De Peralta. 2020. "Do Servant, Transformational, Transactional, And Passive Avoidant Leadership Styles Influence Mentoring Competencies For Faculty? A Study Of A Gender Equity Leadership Development Program". *Human Resource Development Quarterly.* https://doi-org.dbgw.lis.curtin.edu.au/10.1002/hrdq.21408

Skinner, Quentin. 1981. "Machiavelli". *Oxford University Press.* Oxford, New York. https://ap01.alma.exlibrisgroup.com/view/delivery/61CUR_INST/12193963800001951

Spears, Larry. "Reflections on Robert K. Greenleaf and servant-leadership." *Leadership & organization development journal* 17, no. 7 (1996): 33-35. https://www.emerald.com/insight/content/doi/10.1108/01437739610148367/full/html

Stern, Paul. 1999. "Tyranny and Self-Knowledge: Critias and Socrates in Plato's Charmides." *American Political Science Review.* 93 (2): 399–412. https://doi.org/10.2307/2585403

Tao-Nicholson, Rekha, Chris Carr, Stuart Smith. 2020. "Cross-Cultural Leadership Adjustment: A Strategic Analysis Of Expatriate Leadership At A British Multinational Enterprise". *International Business Review* 62 (6): 675-687. https://doi-org.dbgw.lis.curtin.edu.au/10.1002/tie.22176

Taylor, Paul W. 1975. "Principles Of Ethics: An Introduction". *Wadsworth Publishing Company.* Belmont, California.

https://ap01.alma.exlibrisgroup.com/view/delivery/61CUR_INST/12182093390001951

Terblanche, Nicky. 2020. "Coaching Techniques for Sustained Individual Change During Career Transitions". *Human Resource Development Quarterly*. https://doi-org.dbgw.lis.curtin.edu.au/10.1002/hrdq.21405

Tsai, Chin-Ju, Chris Carr, Kun Qiao, Sasiya Supprakit. 2019. "Modes Of Cross Cultural Leadership Adjustment: Adapting Leadership To Meet Local Conditions And/Or Changing Followers To Match Personal Requirements?". *The International Journal of Human Resource Management* 30 (9): 1477-1504. https://doi-org.dbgw.lis.curtin.edu.au/10.1080/09585192.2017.1289549

Walzer, Michael. 1973. "Political Action: The Problem Of Dirty Hands". *Philosophy and Public Affairs* 2 (2): 160-180. https://www.jstor.org/stable/2265139

White, Sarah K. 2022. "What is Servant Leadership? A Philosophy for People-First Leadership". *Executive Network*. https://www.shrm.org/executive-network/insights/servant-leadership-philosophy-people-first-leadership

www.ingramcontent.com/pod-product-compliance
Lightning Source LLC
LaVergne TN
LVHW051602070426
835507LV00021B/2716